Mark Ambrose has provided us with a gift from which we can all learn. *The Will to Love* is an intelligent and evocative reflection on the nature of being human and our capacities to heal ourselves and our world. During these interesting and trying times, we must all be open to *The Will to Love*.

—Dr. Joseph Wise
Chief Education Officer
EdisonLearning

The Will to Love is a spiritual journey with insight and depth. While not specifically parochial, this reflection is essential to anyone trying to better understand themselves, their purpose and desirous to come into contact with the love that creates and sustains us. It is a journey that certainly will keep one asking more questions.

—Father Jerome Borski, OSB
St. Mary's Abbey/Delbarton School

THE
WILL
TO
LOVE

THE WILL TO LOVE

Mark P. Ambrose

TATE PUBLISHING & *Enterprises*

The Will to Love
Copyright © 2009 by Mark P. Ambrose. All rights reserved.

This title is also available as a Tate Out Loud product. Visit www.tatepublishing.com for more information.

No part of this publication may be reproduced, stored in a retrieval system or transmitted in any way by any means, electronic, mechanical, photocopy, recording or otherwise without the prior permission of the author except as provided by USA copyright law.

Scripture quotations marked "RSV" are taken from the *Revised Standard Version of the Bible*, Copyright © 1952 by the Division of Christian Education of the National Council of the Churches of Christ in the United States of American. Used by permission. All rights reserved.

The opinions expressed by the author are not necessarily those of Tate Publishing, LLC.

Published by Tate Publishing & Enterprises, LLC
127 E. Trade Center Terrace | Mustang, Oklahoma 73064 USA
1.888.361.9473 | www.tatepublishing.com

Tate Publishing is committed to excellence in the publishing industry. The company reflects the philosophy established by the founders, based on Psalm 68:11,
"The Lord gave the word and great was the company of those who published it."

Book design copyright © 2009 by Tate Publishing, LLC. All rights reserved.
Cover design by Tyler Evans
Interior design by Nathan Harmony

Published in the United States of America
ISBN: 978-1-60799-839-6
1. Religion: Theology
2. Philosophy: Free Will & Determinism
09.09.29

Dedication

Dedicated to the loving memory of my parents,
Peter and Marilyn, who gave me life,
taught me love, and planted the seeds of my faith.

Acknowledgements

During the course of writing this book, numerous people have provided me their support and their constructive advice. It would be indeed ungrateful to not mention these people now. To William Davies, who endured reading this manuscript multiple times, bringing to it a style and thoughtfulness that have served both the text and me greatly. With thanks to his parents Ruth and William who also read this and provided salient comments throughout. To Father Jerome Borski, OSB, whose multiple meditative readings and spiritual clarity were of unequalled value. To Scott MacDougal, PhD. candidate at Fordham University, whose intense theological debates on certain topics ensured that I stayed attuned to what I was saying and ensured that it was in line with what I meant. To Paul Brennan, whose legal advice ensured my naiveté was kept in appropriate check. Last but not least, thanks to Kalyn McAlister, my chief editor, whose partnership made this work far better as a result of her generous ear and thoughtful mind.

Finally, I would like to acknowledge the many wonderful men who dedicated their lives to striving to live the will to love as Benedictines. Specifically, I would like to express my indebtedness to the monks of St. Mary's Abbey, Delbarton, where I was solemnly professed. It is also essential that I underscore the tremendous influence of the monks of St. Andrew Abbey in Cleveland, Ohio, where I was fortunate to be a novice and junior under a man of incredible authenticity, faith, intelligence, and generosity, Abbot Clement Zeleznik, OSB.

Contents

Foreword	13
Prologue	21
Setting the Goal and Charting a Path	23
The Journey—Its Objective and Outcome	35
Understanding Humanity Through the Creation Myths of the Old Testament	45
Freedom as the Seed of Being Human	59
The Capacities Inherent in Humanity and What They Make Possible	75
Humanity–Space & Time, Abundance & Scarcity	99
The Identity of the Self	113
The Eternal Dance of the "I" and the Other	127

Love—What Does It Mean Within the Context of the "Will"?	143
Love and The New Testament	161
Belief, Faith, and Prayer and Their Meaning in This World	167
The Incarnation—Immanence and Transcendence	183
Sin and Forgiveness in the Will to Love	203
The Will to Love and the Purposeful Life	219
Markers of Avoiding the Purpose-Filled Life	229
Soil and Spirit	237
Conclusion	245

Foreword

A million years ago, as a college sophomore, I discovered the philosophy of Friedrich Nietzsche. More accurately, I discovered one line of the philosophy of Friedrich Nietzsche, hand lettered a cardboard placard with that line, and displayed it over my desk, blithely unaware that every other college sophomore was doing much the same thing at the same time, that thousands of previous college sophomores had already been enlightened, and that thousands more would share my joy in discovering a perfectly sophomoric philosophy of life. Being an intellectually pretentious sophomore and having studied German in high school, I one-upped my classmates by displaying my newfound credo in the original: "*Was mich nicht umbringt macht mich stärker*"—"That which does not destroy me makes me stronger."

It shouldn't surprise anyone that Nietzsche and sophomores are perfect together. The nineteen-year-old, free of parental supervision, free of high school, free of church, synagogue, or mosque, is master of all he surveys, however limited the view. Nietzsche's thinking is a perfect fit. That thinking focuses, essentially, on two things: human will and an assertion that its proper use is the acquisition of power. Nietzsche is certainly not alone among thinkers in emphasizing the importance of human agency and choice: the will. But he rejected the traditional

European assertion—heavily influenced by Christian teaching—that agency and choice should be directed toward helping others, relieving suffering, ensuring peace; activities that Nietzsche, who began life as a philologist, would certainly have enjoyed calling wimpy had the word been available to him. He saw this sort of agency-in-the-service-of-virtue as eviscerating of the human self. Indeed, he saw Christianity as a negative force, inferior, for instance, to the ancient cult of Dionysus, which gave itself over to the gratification of the self. So for Nietzsche, the proper use of will was the pursuit of power and the gratification of the self. What newly liberated kid could resist?

Like most of my fellow nascent existentialists, I grew out of it.

Here is a book that does something more useful with Nietzsche than wallowing in him; it takes him on. "The Will to Love is a direct assault on Nietzsche's *Will to Power*," says the author, and a good thing too. For, while Nietzsche himself may not be widely read, his best known aphorism is a totem to a way of thinking that has had a profound effect during the last hundred years of human history.

Nietzsche's *Will to Power* was his last book, published posthumously, in 1909. Its publication date already suggests its significance, born as it was in that netherworld of *fin de siècle* Europe, a Europe standing on the precipice of World War I, but not yet fully aware of the horror into which it was about to leap. Indeed, the British war poet Rupert Brooke could hardly wait to jump into the glory of war, a war he saw as potentially cathartic for the continent, a war into which its young men would plunge, "as swimmers into cleanness leaping." One version of the origin of Nietzsche's philosophy suggests that his devotion to will and power was born on the battlefields of the Franco-Prussian War, and both Brooke and Nietzsche brought to the pre-war period an essentially nineteenth century point of view: War was a glorious source of honor and manhood; the exercise of power was essential to national interests; nationalism and patriotism were the premier virtues ("Dulce et decorum est, pro patria mori" had not yet been condemned as a lie). The realities of the trenches changed all that for the men who leapt into them and found not cleanness, but misery, filth, disease, violence, and death. They don't call it a *fin de siècle* for nothing.

It would be nice to think that the patriotic gore of the twentieth century's first Great War killed off Nietzschean devotion to the will to power as well. A quick perusal of the list of post-World War I European leaders suggests otherwise. Stalin, Franco (with his Portuguese neighbor Salazar), Mussolini, and Hitler all gloried in the will to power and transformed it, for awhile at least, into a workable geopolitical strategy, more successful in the 1930s (by the measures of wealth and dominion, anyway) than the more tender democratic systems they derided. While the democratic nations stalled in economic depression, the totalitarian states appeared to offer a working alternative. That these states professed to offer their citizens a Nietzschean solution based in a radical assertion of individual agency was, however, an exercise in sleight of hand. Both Stalinist Marxism and Nazi Fascism were based in determinisms that subjugated the individual to the state. Ironically, the vaunting hubris of the great dictators could be shared in only by deriving one's agency through membership in the Party and by sacrificing one's individuality to the eventual achievement of the Classless Society or the Thousand Year Reich.

Two wars—one hot, one cold—occupied the second half of the twentieth century. World War II came about as close as any war can to being a battle between good and evil. The good for which the Allies fought was essentially saving individual rights from being crushed by totalitarian systems. The process of defeating Nazi Germany in Europe and Imperial Japan in Asia brought with it revelations of the depths of evil to which totalitarian systems can sink: the holocaust and the rape of Nanking spring to mind (both based in odious theories of racial superiority), but anyone who has read the most rudimentary of histories could extend the list of atrocities. The inextricable interconnection of totalitarianism and loss of individuality (and even of humanity) taught the victorious powers the virtue of vigilance in opposing threats to individual rights when finally the democratic nations were victorious in 1945.

Except that one of the victorious nations wasn't democratic. The Grand Alliance—the US, Britain, and the USSR—was perhaps less a grand one than an alliance of necessity. The cracks within the façade of unity were evident in almost every wartime meeting, but especially toward the end in meetings at Yalta and Potsdam, and they opened into chasms as soon as World War II was won. Increasingly, the incompatibility of democratic and totalitarian systems became evident in disputes over the fate of territories recently held by German forces and of Germany itself. Very quickly, the hot war just ended was replaced by a cold war, one that would stretch over the next fifty years. Both sides retreated to their respective corners, declaring the world a bipolar one in which every nation must choose up sides, joining either the Soviet orbit or that of what soon became known as the Free World, with the US as its leader. Again each side clung to opposing ideologies, one based in individual freedoms and one in social, political, and economic control.

This great bipolar divide defined both foreign and domestic politics on both sides of what Winston Churchill famously called the Iron Curtain. From 1949 forward, both great powers had harnessed the atom and piled up bombs aimed at each other. For most of the period, domestic political foes could be easily bested if tarred with the brush of communism in the west or bourgeois corruption in the east. Each side's political identity became weirdly tied by a negative political mathematics to the other's. To be a loyal American was not to be a communist. (Oaths were produced and taken to prove it.) To be a valiant Soviet comrade was not to be seduced by the empty promises of capitalism. (The oaths and proofs were often skipped in favor of a few brisk winters east of the Urals for those who fell to such seductions.) Neither ideological center ever attacked the other militarily, despite coming perilously close during a few famous days in the autumn of 1962. They preferred to fight proxy wars, seeing each other's puppets at work in Africa, Latin America, the Middle East, and Asia, funneling arms and spies to the appropriate places—exercising the will to power through the agency of others. And then, over the space of a few short years in the late '80s and early '90s, the long struggle ended.

For those who are too young to have experienced the Cold War, it is hard to comprehend how sudden its end seemed. The collapse of the eastern bloc—symbolized in the frenzy of joy with which Europe celebrated the opening of the Berlin Wall—and finally of the Soviet Union itself came as a shock to those for whom the essential opposition of the two systems of thought and government seemed as fundamentally a part of life as the law of gravity. We had won (or at least they had lost), and it seemed too good to be true. Which, of course, it was.

The fighting of wars—hot or cold—draws battle lines in a comfortingly clear manner. No one ever rallied the troops by demanding that they form up and consider the intricacies of philosophy. Once the enemy is gone, though, we are left with the problem of defining the nature of the victory. What, exactly, has triumphed, and what has been vanquished? The question is particularly profound when our very sense of ourselves has been so influenced by the sort of negative definition mentioned above. We are not communists! The thing is, neither are they, now, so the punch has rather gone out of the self-concept. For more than half a century, western societies and governments had embraced the fight for individualism. The waning and final defeat of the anti-individualist system against which they had defined themselves would seem to have left open a field in which individual talent and initiative—untrammeled human agency—could flower. If freedom had now triumphed, freedom to do *what*? Communism had not brought us down, but had the fighting of it made us stronger?

The celebration of individualism had a sort of double incarnation in the last days of the Cold War in a famous political non-couple: Margaret Thatcher and Ronald Reagan. Each expressed an unshakable faith in the possibilities of the individual freed from the restraints of government. Each is famously remembered for expressing that faith. "Government is not the solution," said Reagan, "it is the problem." Prime Minister Thatcher put it more bluntly. "There is no such thing as society," she said, "only individuals." Such was the reigning orthodoxy in the west as the Cold War came to an end. And so it was that orthodoxy that seemed vindicated by the end of the Soviet Union, with its command economy and disregard for individual rights. Individual agency—the will—was triumphant once again.

The triumph of the will, however, left the greater part of the question unanswered; or, perhaps, answered in the default position of Nietzsche: the best use of the will is the acquisition of power. In the case of the post-Cold War west, acquisition was, indeed, the name of the game. The new heroes were corporate officials in charge of mergers and acquisitions. If there were proxy wars, they were in stockholder meetings. No figure was more romantic than a hedge fund manager. We all know, of course, that merging and acquiring—to say nothing of hedging—have not turned out entirely as those who put their faith in the triumph of individualism promised. Radical individualism—the will to power—often, if not inevitably, leads to the pursuit of ends that disregard the broader interests of the society within which the individual lives. Buying and selling bundles of debt can certainly make some individuals rich and powerful, but it can also leave others without houses.

It was the English philosopher Thomas Hobbes who insisted that humans were engines of self-interest who would stop at nothing to gain their ends. His was not an optimistic philosophy and it is hard to imagine Hobbes having a light moment. Still, one cannot help wondering whether he is currently chortling up his sleeve at the damage done by the rampant individualism of the last twenty years or so. Rugged individualism looks a lot less attractive when things get really rugged.

And so we find ourselves, almost a decade into the twenty-first century, again confronting the question of will, of human agency. The great value of *The Will to Love* is that it refrains from merely following the pendulum in a swing back to the assertion of societal interests in the face of individualism. Rather, it sticks with the question of will, but answers directly Nietzsche's claim that its proper object is power. The will to power hasn't done much for humanity in the last century. The assertion implicit in the title of this volume is that love is the more valid goal of human agency, that the will to *power* must be replaced by the will to *love*.

At this point a warning to potential readers seems warranted. If you have picked up this book in the hope of finding anodyne phrases for troubled times, put it down now. This is not an easy book, not so much in the sense of intellectual difficulty, but in the sense that it is hard to imagine any reader turning the last page without having had some cherished idea challenged. The same thing, of course, could be said of the Bible—unless you read it assuming you already know what it all means.

So who *should* read on? If you grew up with a religious faith, but have the feeling it didn't grow up with you, you should keep reading. If you are of a certain age and remember when *love* was a word charged with political meaning, keep reading—no matter which side of love your politics put you on. If you have the vague sense that agency and meaning are in some way connected (that is that what one does has some necessary connection to one's sense of the purposefulness of one's life), plunge ahead. If you are either a religious conservative or a religious liberal, but would like to move beyond those labels, continue. If you are suspicious of religions but think there might be something in religion, you are another candidate for the whole volume. Finally, if you once thought you had found the key to life's meaning in a single assertion of German self-will, you really should keep reading.

William G. Davies
Head, Department of History
Hackley School
Tarrytown, New York

(William Davies holds a BA in history from Bowdoin College, an MA in theology from The Catholic University of America, and spent a year reading theology and history at St. Benet's Hall of Oxford University.)

God's Grandeur

The world is charged with the grandeur of God
It will flame out, like shining from shook foil;
It gathers to a greatness, like the ooze of oil
Crushed. Why do men then now not reck his rod?
Generations have trod, have trod, have trod;
And all is seared with trade; bleared, smeared with toil;
And wears man's smudge and shares man's smell: the soil
Is bare now, nor can foot feel being shod.

And for all this, nature is never spent
There lives the dearest freshness deep down things;
And though the last lights off the black West went
Oh, morning, at the brown brink eastward, springs—
Because the Holy Ghost over the bent
World broods with warm breast and with ah! bright wings
—Gerard Manley Hopkins
(1844–1889)

Prologue

It is very important to know up front what type of book this is and what type of book it is not. *The Will to Love* is not meant to be a novel, mystery, romance, self-help, or academic text. This is a reflection based on personal observations and experiences about life, humanity, and spirituality. It carries within it the influences of my academic background in philosophy, theology, and spirituality. *The Will to Love* emerges from my journey that has taken me from being a solemnly professed Benedictine monk to a member of our secular society. It is a book that I have felt called to write and that has been long in the process of being born. While it has as its core a Judeo-Christian perspective, it is universal in its message and, I hope, in its applicability.

I have become increasingly convinced that at humanity's spiritual center, the truth wears no particular costume and is a slave to no culture, creed, or set of traditions. Each person who approaches this book will bring to it her own history, unique experiences, thoughts, and reflections concerning existence, purpose, and ultimately their individual meaning. It is my firm desire that each individual perspective will be enhanced by and added to through the process of engaging this reflection. Most of all, it is my deepest desire to enhance each reader's sense of the multi-textured richness and wonder that is his life.

This is a book for those who thirst to discover themselves and the meaning of the precious gift of their lives. I chose a reflection as the form for this book based on my Benedictine background and my belief that reflection is the most appropriate method for reacquiring ourselves at the myriad levels of our existence. It does not postulate a narrow path, rather it requests of readers to have the courage to entertain questions and to choose their paths with greater insight and consciousness. I hope this book is seen as unequivocally inclusive as it asks each reader to meditate and reflect on the universal aspects of living, striving, and ultimately accepting the central role of mystery in all things, especially ourselves.

It is my fervent prayer that this reflection will enrich your own appreciation of life in general and your own life experienced and chosen individually. I also hope and pray that the result of this intimate exchange will make the reader fundamentally capable of hearing the many calls from God to be his* arms and legs, ears and voice as he seeks fully to exploit your unique being for the healing of our world and each other. I believe that we live in important times and that each person is an essential player in transforming our world and changing its trajectory. No one is insignificant. No one is outside the loving embrace of God and his desire for us to develop into the fullness of our beings.

May this sharing, with its ultimate call to action for each of us, bring us true peace, a realized sense of purpose, and an opening of our spirits to ourselves, to each other, and to the Spirit that gives, sustains, and is life.

*The use of the masculine gender when referring to God is being chosen to facilitate the notion of God as *Father* and his relational reality. Later, the Holy Spirit is referred to as the generative facet of the Father and thus female.

Setting the Goal and Charting a Path

What is the meaning of being human in the twenty-first century? Is it more or less difficult than it has been in all the centuries that have preceded it? If one cannot determine objectively whether it is more difficult to be a fulfilled human being today than in any other period of time, then are there unique challenges that being a Christian entails in this, our time? There are unique challenges for the disciples of Jesus today that are both material and foundational. These foundational challenges result from the fact that being a Christian is based on a particular view of what it means to be human and that this understanding is anything but clear to many in this modern world.

Contemporary concepts that undergird what it means to be human, what humans are both capable of and, therefore, potentially responsible for, have been radically altered from the basic notion of humanity upon which the core of Christianity was built. Our modern unquestioned beliefs in science and the mechanistic view of our world and our very selves, as well as the unquestioned notion that the human mind can grasp and explain anything, given time, are examples of some major changes. Consider, if you will, our present use of the word "mind." For many, "mind" has become synonymous with "brain." This is an assumption not only not validated, but also seriously restricting in terms of much richer meanings and capacities that one might be willing to attribute to the mind and not to the brain. While certainly few would argue that the brain has a significant role in our capacity to live and express many of our faculties, it is a mistake, however, to make the leap that many of our capacities are reducible to specific operations of the brain. Specifically, functions such as consciousness have never been proven to be a faculty of the brain, though few would argue that our capacity to express our consciousness relies on many functions controlled directly by the brain. These revised views of humanity and the world are outcomes of a view of the world that is mechanical, rational, ordered, and predictable and that the apparent chaos of life is only the result of our present inability to grasp the multitude of factors that make each outcome necessary. It is thus a worldview in which human freedom is at best an outmoded notion reminiscent of a romantic past. For if such a concept as freedom were to really exist, it would be so severely constrained by our chemical makeup, the environments we were born into, and our genetic programming that any meaningful sense of the word would be lost.

The ideas of truth, justice, right, and wrong have also ceased to be objectively meaningful for many, and in many cases are considered the arbitrary outcomes of communal agreements, which decree a set of rules for its members that are sometimes justified by communities merely based on their utility. We live in a time when the mystery of each person is often experienced as a deficiency that can be overcome through continued scientific investigation into the biological components that make us up and the specific knowledge of the experiences that have colored our lives.

This is a reexamination of the modern notion of the human person. This reflection entails a meditative review of many of our modern accepted ideas of humanity and the world in which we live. It is an attempt to assess our modern views in terms of their sufficiency in accounting for the many aspects of our experiences, capacities, and complexities, as well as their ability to explain many of the unique potentialities that dwell at the very core of our beings. It is a reaffirmation of a concept of the human person in opposition to modern materialistic reductionism. It seeks to reaffirm the nature of humanity based on the Judeo-Christian tradition. It will reaffirm humanity's wonder and awe, mystery and capacity. It will pronounce a view of humanity that is radically free and thus radically responsible and accountable. As such, this reflection will articulate a meaning of being human that can sustain the call of Jesus and the mission of salvation that each one of us has been challenged to effect.

As part of this reclamation of our identity, our capacity, and our potential, this reflection will focus upon our possibilities as human beings and the full meaning of the Christian message as both the fulfillment of our creation and the basis of our salvation. This is a reflection about what it means to achieve the full potential of our humanity. It is an attempt to stand back from the frenetic lives we live and to ponder who we are. In raising the question of "who I am?" as well as of "who I would like to be?" and "who am I capable of being?" this reflection will ponder some of the most significant questions that any individual can ask. It will require that each person who takes this journey pause and reflect not on one's career, one's many roles (as father, mother, sister, brother, etc.), but on looking within and ascertaining where one is on the path to fullness of life. This reflection is itself the outcome of such a journey, taken within a Christian context, over many years. It is a sharing of one person's path to self-possession, knowledge, insight, humility, and a capacity to love as each of us has already been loved. It is by no means a finished process, but one to which we seek to be more committed today than each day that preceded this one.

This is a ruminating on the insights from numerous sources

without an attempt to be encyclopedic or purely academic in nature. Its focus is therefore more in the tradition of the monastic concept of *lectio divina* (meditating on the divine Word). It entails the reading, ruminating, and resulting lifelong lingering on the text within the soul of the monk. As the monk continues to live his life, the seed that is planted via the text in his soul, and upon which he continuously contemplates, grows and expands as it is watered by the experiences and challenges of his life lived in community. It is within this lived context that the Word of the text becomes vital and is able to transform both the individual monk and, in turn, the community within which he lives. Unlike its use in the more limited monastic context, this articulation will not use Scripture as its sole source, for it takes a wider view of *lectio,* based on the belief that insight, indeed *truth,* can be found in many sources and that any soul open to truth should not be surprised to find it in the strangest of places. In fact, a fundamental presupposition will be that truth is no individual's, religion's, government's, or community's unique possession.

For millennia, great thinkers have been affirming that humanity has a nature. Some, like Plato, Augustine, and Freud, have proposed that humanity's nature is brutish, broken, and in need of being made right. How they chose to make it right was, in part, based on their belief systems and worldviews.

Plato's philosophy clearly distinguished warring elements within each human person and thus a political model that would ensure that those most in control of the less noble aspects of their natures would be in charge. These philosopher-kings would set up educational institutions and political communities meant to bring humanity to its highest fulfillment.

Augustine, in coherence with platonic ideas, now transformed by his Christian conversion, formalized the notion of humanity's warring elements into his idea of concupiscence—humanity's underlying tendency toward evil; seen by Augustine as a direct result of Adam and Eve's disobedience to God in paradise, which he calls original sin. For this reason, Augustine mandated that infants be baptized as soon as possible to protect them from the "cost of sin" even before they could actually commit sin. For, in Augustine's theology, the infant is not sinless. The infant already is marked with the sin of Adam and must therefore be baptized and washed with the salvific waters of redemption if it is to be saved.

Freud, unlike his two predecessors, was an Enlightenment thinker and certainly not a Platonist in a strict sense (though one could argue for the influence of platonic concepts in his thought). He developed a notion of humanity that was also in need of control. Freud's tripartite division of human nature into the id, ego, and super-ego was the profound announcement to the modern world of our unconscious selves. The id, which was both energy and unconscious self, gave birth to the understanding of the individual as both unknown and, in some regard, not responsible. In the nineteenth century, Robert Louis Stevenson had written a novel that prefigured this concept of the id, or dark side of humanity, in *Dr. Jekyll and Mr. Hyde*. Stevenson depicts Dr. Jekyll as a kindly man who attempts to find a formula that can isolate the evil core within humanity. Unfortunately, he unleashes this evil core within himself. Many centuries later, this same concept of an inner demon would again be referenced in a sitcom of the 1960s with the now famous line, "The devil made me do it." This idea of an inner unconscious self that is unknown, powerful, base, and in dire need of control has permeated our sense of who we are, what we can expect of ourselves, how we create societies, how we should treat those who commit crimes, and how we educate our children. It is in many respects a key element of the nature/nurture argument that still rages in various forms today.

In opposition to the view of humanity as depraved or in some way broken, there have been those who have held that humanity is inherently good, or at least neutral, and that it is society itself that corrupts this perfect nature each time a child is brought into the world. Thomas Aquinas, Rousseau, Spinoza, and Locke are all examples of thinkers who believed in the inherent goodness of humanity. They fully believed that if a person were kept on the right course and not deformed by external events, he/she would blossom forth with all the best qualities of his or her nature. Aquinas refused to believe, as Augustine had, that between God and man there was an unbridgeable chasm. He saw Augustine's desire to denigrate humanity in order to exalt God's immutable perfection as a false dichotomy. Humanity in the eyes of Aquinas was the pinnacle of God's creative acts. In fact, humanity's potential, contrary to diminishing God's supremacy and glory, was viewed as actually demonstrating God's glory in one of its most perfect ways. It was for this reason that God chose the human condition as the ultimate vehicle through which to redeem all of creation.

Rousseau accepted that each person was born into the human condition purely good and that experience should only enrich and deepen a person's already wondrous gifts. Rousseau's fervent belief in liberty as the necessary pre-requisite to any person's achieving their positive potential was a key to understanding his abhorrence of tyranny wherever it showed its face. For it was this tyranny that malformed and made monsters of us all. Humanity has, for Rousseau, natural rights, and these require protection from tyranny so that the right order of our natures can be expressed.

Spinoza, a philosopher and rationalist, believed that there was not good or bad, evil or sin without society. He believed that humanity, in a state of nature, was above these categories. Humans, Spinoza believed, were desirous of their survival. Inherently, humanity is neither bad nor good; humans are just what they are. For Spinoza, moral categories such as good and evil are later accretions which society layers onto the human condition.

John Locke, the famous English philosopher and member of the empirical school, believed that humanity in a "state of nature" was at peace and was intelligent and good. Locke believed that humanity was born empty of ideas, a *tabula rasa*—a blank slate. As an empiricist, he believed that through experiences (both the five senses and a close look at the experiences that followed from these), people came to knowledge and understanding of themselves and their world. For Locke, government was the prerogative of equals to contract together to create a structure for humanity's mutual service and proper unfolding.

These diverse views of humanity's nature yielded and still yield real outcomes, e. g. structures of societies, our notion of law and punishment, and the role of education, to name but a few. If one starts with the belief that humanity is bad or evil, control and manipulation through education, laws, and the use of deterrents such as publicly prescribed punishments, including death, may be appropriate outcomes. The objective for this negative view of humanity's nature is the proper control of the individual as well as the protection of society.

If humans are inherently selfish and brutish, as was the opinion of Thomas Hobbes, then human beings should contract together for their own best interest. By this social contract, we will be in a better position to meet our own selfish needs of nourishment, procreation, protection, and advancement. Society is thus the pragmatic aggregation of humanity for the taming of our own natures for our own best interest.

In opposition to this theory, if one begins with the view of humanity as inherently good and equal, as did Hobbes' countryman John Locke, society is the coming together for the purpose of protecting the natural rights of humanity. It is ensuring that humanity's nature is given the correct soil in which to flower and grow and thus supports a concept of education, which elicits the qualities of the person within. It is within this context that the notion of a liberal education, *i.e.*, an education that would free the inner spirit, makes sense. Democracy is a concept at home with a notion of humanity as good and noble. It is no wonder then that Plato thought democracy the worst form of government.

All of the characterizations of humanity in its "state of nature" presented above are over-generalizations, but should give a sense of how essential one's starting point is to the view of the person, society, the role of government, education, religion, and morality that follows from these perspectives. Both the positive and the negative view of humanity are meant to provide a broad appreciation for the fact that the foundational view of humanity one accepts will significantly influence the Christian interpretation that rests on top of it.

The perspective of this work will veer away from a static notion of human nature and dwell more on human capacities and agency. Specifically, the core of this rumination will be targeted at humanity's freedom rather than on a belief in its deterministic nature. In the nineteenth century, there was great emphasis on the nature of man. If humanity has a nature, our perspective will be that each person's nature is to be free to discover and become one's self through the proper exercise of one's *will*. We will posit that humanity is, therefore, not merely free, but radically free. Another critical aspect of the definition of freedom is that our freedom is something that we exercise even when we choose not to. Thus our freedom is an essential and inescapable aspect of our beings that is and will be exercised despite our potential unconscious awareness. The implications and meaning of this concept of freedom will be one of the major themes that will permeate this entire reflection. This foundational premise of radical freedom is represented in the concept of will, which is—*The Will to Love*.

The exercise of discerning who each of us is and what our life is or is not about is inescapable. The question is whether each of us will choose our life or make the choice to not choose and what effect this decision to abdicate my conscious choice might have on me and all those I claim to love.

The discovery of purpose comes from our status as conscious and free beings, as well as from our call to participate in life as a process and not as a conveyer belt of forward motion that makes the past determinative of who I am for the remainder of my life. Purpose is as fundamental to humanity as is the freedom that is at its core. Freedom and purpose entail responsibility, accountability, and meaning. These concepts will be central to this examination of humanity.

How has humanity used its capabilities, capacities, and freedom in terms of its ability to grow and improve itself and its world? This question links abstract anthropology to the concrete realities of human existence. Humanity's recorded history, if considered in terms of collective achievements, could certainly be described as a series of tremendous peaks and valleys. Periods of great achievement are abundant and could be grouped according to innumerable themes—political, cultural, intellectual, scientific, religious, aesthetic, medical, technological, sociological, psychological. Equally deep troughs or periods of decline also characterize humanity's history. These periods represent times in which it has appeared that humanity has devolved or lost its way and as a result has become all that is least noble. Holding these highly abstract patterns aside, the real question of importance is, have humans improved as a species over this great expanse of our time on this earth? Narrowing this time period somewhat, could we really say that humanity has fundamentally become nobler in the last two thousand years?

There are many ways to confront this question. The method used here will focus on humanity's internal transformations rather than its abilities to transform externals. It would be hard to deny humanity's unique capacities to adapt externals to accommodate itself to its surroundings. Humanity's ability to use its mind and imagination to create undreamt-of capabilities not only to ensure its survival, but to facilitate its complete dominance over almost every aspect of the world in which it dwells is a fundamental manifestation of its unique manner of being. The real question is and has always been whether humanity has the same capacity to develop and evolve its inner self.

Is there any proof that humanity in the twenty-first century is inherently any nobler, any more generous of spirit, any less cruel, less self-preoccupied than its ancestors, who destroyed the temple in Jerusalem, crucified Jesus, sacked Rome, slaughtered thousands in the Crusades, tortured untold numbers in the Inquisition, Holocaust, Rwanda, and countless other atrocities? If humanity is not appreciably better, what does this say about us? What does it say of all the prophets of God: Mohammad, Buddha, Jesus, and the all the great religions such as Zoroastrianism, Confucianism, Hinduism, and Buddhism that have called forth humanity's more noble natures? Have all these messages been for naught? Is it possible that the message of Christianity itself has failed? If not, what has happened, and can humanity's spirit be reinvigorated?

Humanity in the twenty-first century appears to be adrift. Nietzsche claimed in the nineteenth century that "God is dead," and men cringed. Many saw this outrageous statement as scandalous, sacrilegious, and unacceptable. In point of fact, Nietzsche described a transformation that had little to do with the reality of the divine but everything to do with our societies and the underlying values that were apparent to those willing to see and apprehend. His *Will to Power* was a natural outgrowth of the world in which humanity was now God. The concept of the *superman* was in many respects the necessary replacement for what Nietzsche perceived to be the projection of humanity's ultimate capabilities on a mythological deity long expired.

Many of the radical ideas of Nietzsche and those that followed him have continued to play themselves out in our modern world even as many still claim to hold Judeo-Christian values. In fact, a central theme is that the crisis of our age is, in part, an outcome of the *Will to Power*, which continues to play out in the modern world. This outcome has passed beyond the death of God and is now positioning for the potential death of humanity itself.

The death of humanity does not require humanity's physical annihilation, nor is it a foregone conclusion. Unfortunately, though, many of its symptoms are already familiar to modern society. It can be characterized by the slow euthanizing of humanity's spirit. It is manifest by an ever-increasing willingness to exist in a state of semi-consciousness. Its characteristics are in humanity's willingness to abandon those things historically held most dear, such as freedom, life, one's beliefs, justice, concern for the downtrodden, hope for a better tomorrow, a desire to leave something behind. In its place can be seen an unquenchable need to acquire, to hoard, and the avoidance of freedom and truth with their corresponding virtues of responsibility and accountability. Our increased facility to not see, hear, or notice, as well as a profound lack of courage, called cynicism, and the underlying but pervasive fear which infects so many of our individual and communal actions, grows and distorts any ability to address so many of our social and political issues.

The Will to Love is a direct assault on Nietzsche's *Will to Power*. It is a cry to remember who we are. It is a set of reflections whose *raison d'être*, or reason to be, is to poke and prod us to reassess our deepest natures and to be open to the possible reassessment of the core purposes of our lives. It is about opening up the questions of who we are and what we are called to be. It questions the deterministic and materialistic views that many have accepted about our world and ourselves. It posits a radical responsibility and accountability for who we are and will be. It also proclaims vigorously that happiness, peace, and fulfillment in this world are not just possible, but are what we are meant to have. In the end, this is a call to action. It is meant to evoke thought and discussion, but if this is all it does, it is a failure. Its hope is to be a cause of change, to encourage renewal, an awakening of the spirit within each of us. It is meant to inspire hope and a sense of orientation for oneself and for all those who inwardly strive for something better.

The Journey— Its Objective and Outcome

The desire to understand oneself, one's relationship to the world, others, and God is basic to every person. Unfortunately for many, these relationships, which often present themselves to us as questions, are resolved in the light of other people's or society's prejudices. In some cases, these core concerns are demoted to the pure emotional reaction against many of those who have chosen not to respond authentically, thus appearing hypocritical to their purported beliefs as indicated in their responses to the personal challenges each of us face. In this context, some choose lives of internal and external desperation that poison the communities in which we all live and struggle.

The cynic, the bitter, and often those who hide behind their position or power are examples of individuals who have aggressively decided to avoid the difficult questions that are raised herein. Cynicism is a prominent fixture in our culture and is particularly effective at coloring almost any experience. This cynicism leaves its victims as mere observers along the sidelines of life. The objects of the cynic's rage can be almost anything—religion, political parties, not-for-profit organizations, you name it. Usually the organizations focused on are striving to bring men and women of goodwill closer to the truth of themselves and each other in some way. The cynic's posture is always as the third party, far enough away not to be affected and focusing on the imperfections of those seeking and striving to be better, but who are, in the eyes of the eternal sideline critic, merely hypocritical and naïve. It is so much easier to focus on the faults and limitations of others than to face oneself, who one is and how one's life is affecting this world through one's participation in it.

Certainly, those who stand on the sidelines of life pointing out the imperfections of others cannot be faulted in many of their perceptions. Every human organization has the faults and frailties that humanity brings to it. Certainly the cynic may be able to list specific individuals who practice a faith and yet who also manifest their human frailty and weakness. Specific to religions, this posture of disdain, based on the imperfections of the humanity of the members of any faith community, is rooted in a fundamental confusion. The spiritual realities that underpin sincere religious traditions and their creeds are the goals for which each of us strives. Different religions have a variety of practices that are meant to lead us to the "holy." The religious traditions and methods that are at the heart of various rituals and practices are the expressions of the unique paths that each religion has developed to aid its members in bringing the community of followers closer to the center, the holy. Religions are not institutions where the perfect are set in place to judge others. Nor is the imperfection of human beings a reason for not participating in the search for the sacred and its meanings, which are integral to the complete natures of our lives. Religions, which are based on various creeds, are the human expressions of the symbols that enable people of faith to both express their experience of the sacred and to be fed by the sacred. Christianity is comprised of numerous religions, but is constituted of one common faith. The different manifestations of religious communities are expressive of various human responses to that common faith. While the underlying core beliefs are common, there are, for many reasons, multiple expressions of these common beliefs, which are the human responses based on historical, theological, and human attractions to various alternative expressions.

A fundamental first principle in understanding ourselves as humans is to appreciate the fact that we are fundamentally creatures who know and express ourselves through symbols. Words, whether spoken or written, are symbols. A flower offered to a loved one, a hug, a smile—these are all examples of symbols, whose function is to bridge the gap between us. Humans create, discover, pass on, and make symbols as an essential aspect of our beings. Symbols are not accidental aspects of human existence, but essential methods for communicating, for creating and expressing meaning and bridging the chasm of our individuality, which can ameliorate the isolation that would make our individuality a tortuous prison from which escape would almost be impossible.

Symbols that attempt to express our experiences of or desire to communicate with the sacred will be referred to as sacraments. Sacraments are those symbols that humans come to invest with a special quality. A symbol is the meaning we can give to something external such as a rose, a word, a hug, or a laugh to express an internal reality externally in order to share with others. A sacrament is a symbol that goes beyond bridging the chasm between individuals or communities and attempts to bridge the gap between the divine and the human. Ritual, liturgy, and prayer use symbols in this special way and are often elevated to the level of a sacrament. A symbol becomes a sacrament when that which it seeks to make present to oneself or another is the sacred or ineffable Other that we seek to experience, praise, and worship in various ways and traditions.

The word sacrament has very specific meanings for certain religions such as Orthodox Christians, Roman Catholics, and other communities of faith. It is essential that it be clear that its use in this context is much more general and less refined so that it could be understood more broadly and yet express the richness of its meaning. Religion, no matter the creed, is the formalization of practices and rituals with symbols and sacraments for the sole purpose of providing the space for God and his creatures to meet. Membership in a religion is not based on perfection, therefore, but rather on shared common beliefs, faith, and hope, as well as shared symbols and sacraments.

This concept of specific symbols relevant to spiritual spaces is very important for us to grasp. In his book *Considering Transcendence*, Martin De Nys, makes clear that even our language takes on unique rules when one is addressing or describing the sacred and our experiences with the sacred. The sacred is most often discussed within the language of metaphor and poetry. This in no way is a comment on its veracity, but rather the realization that our grasp of the sacred is not the same as our grasp of an everyday experience. Traditionally there has always been an appreciation of this within theology as expressed in the concepts of ascending and descending theology.

Ascending theology is speaking about the sacred from our human experience. These articulations are indicative of our experiences of the sacred and thus really focus on our attempt to give expression to that which is much larger than our capacities about which to make literal claims. For this reason, metaphor and poetic language have enabled the richness of these experiences to be articulated without losing the richness and texture they involve and evoke. Descending theology is an attempt to study the sacred from a top down view. The *via negativa*, or "negative way," was the theological realization that nothing we say about God can be literally true, for God is beyond human concepts. For this reason descending theology has usually made use of discussing what God is not, or using *supra*, or "above," in front of any descriptor.

The capacity of formulating questions such as "Who am I?" or

"What is my life all about?" or "Is there any meaning behind all of this?" requires the awareness of one's entire being and the capacity for reflecting on one's own experiences. It is not, therefore, something typically achieved at a particular moment or in the blush of one's youth. These questions are part of the process of the journey of life. Each of us will answer these fundamental questions in ways that evolve over time, whether we do it consciously or not. The role of our conscious will, reason, and judgment in the formulation of our answers to these and many such central questions is often far less than one might imagine. This frightening fact is even more woeful if one considers that from these answers, consciously or unconsciously formulated, evolve one's character, one's ethics, indeed one's entire worldview.

As we journey through this adventure, making our fundamental choices explicit and placing them in the context of our vocations will allow us to assess where we are on our journey through life as human beings, as well as our journey toward the sacred. This journey toward the sacred, it will become apparent, is not a separate path from the journey that is paramount to one's unfolding identity, but the convergence and integration of an individual's identity into an authentic self.

I am not proposing to assess every possible aspect of who we are and our place in this world and our potential purposes and possibilities, but rather to expose and question many of the accepted views of humanity with an eye toward revealing their inadequacy and potential pitfalls. The perspective offered is certainly a slanted one, though not a parochial one. It is a Christian perspective capable of being meaningful to anyone seeking to understand the secrets of a fulfilled life. It is *not* a fundamentalist point of view, nor is it a highly academic point of view. It is built on a strong tradition given voice by Anselm of Canterbury when he said that all theology should be "faith seeking understanding."

This posture of St. Anselm's is critical to keep in mind as the method being taken here. I am making no claims at describing God's designs or ways of interacting with us, his creatures, as he alone knows them. This is well beyond the grasp of mere mortals. This reflection is taking a different starting point. It starts with the position that we can, through consideration of realities not outside of our proper scope, come to a coherent understanding of who we are and how we fit into salvation history without reducing God to something other than God and without robbing humanity of its freedom. The results of this approach will not and cannot answer every nuance of this most ineffable of relationships, between God and his creatures, but it can cause us to embrace a more textured and mature participation in the relationship that is there.

Within this context, this is a meditation on the larger questions: Who are we (human beings)? Why are we here? What is our purpose in living? What should our expectations of life be? Is happiness what we should be seeking? If not happiness, what else? What is freedom, or is it an illusion? What are belief and faith? What is the purpose and meaning of prayer? Is there a God and, if so, how can he not be guilty of incomprehensible evil? What is the role of mystery in life or is this just theological claptrap? What is the extent of human responsibility in salvation history and what, if anything, does it have to do with my everyday choices? By no means are these all the questions. They do, however, encompass the majority of the terrain. These questions are essential questions that are at the center of every person's process of living, no matter how they are dealt with or disposed of.

We should never stop assessing who we are and where we stand in our progression to becoming Christian. Life continues to challenge our perspectives, and, to the degree that we are open, life asks us to continually reformulate our presuppositions about who we are and how we look at our world and our role within it, in light of new experiences from both within and without. Salvation, both our own and the world's, is dependent on our ability to be startled from old ways of being, perceiving, and interacting. In periods of uncertainty, we should be open to the possibility of new insights, which reformulate the way we perceive, respond to, and live within our world and our views of ourselves, our neighbors, and our God.

Another critical point to make as we begin this journey concerns the notion of myth, which is used throughout. The concept of myth being used here is not novel, but it is specific. By myth is meant a story used to tell a fundamental truth. To quote D. H. Lawrence, "Myth is an attempt to narrate a whole human experience, of which the purpose is too deep, going too deep in the blood and soul, for mental explanation or description." The specifics of a myth are used to convey a truth, but may not be important in conveying evidentiary details.

Myth was a popular mechanism for a community's articulation of its identity before the invention of cheap paper and the printing press. It provided not just the communication of shared meanings and symbols to future generations but also a tool for remembering via the very method used to enshrine these truths, meanings, and symbols. This notion of truth-telling was far more prevalent in societies associated with the writers of both the Old and New Testaments. Our modern methods of writing are quite different. Our need to use the method of communication as a tool, in lieu of the prevalence of paper, pencil, and publishing houses, changes not only what we focus on but also how we communicate what needs to be communicated. The plethora of other communication vehicles that we have added to writing and speaking only distances us further from the conditions of the ancient writers and their challenges. The texts of these authors must, therefore, be approached with a different perspective and an appreciation of their task.

This uniqueness of historical method can and does lead to problems in the engagement of not only biblical texts but any ancient text as well. This is important to emphasize at this juncture so that when a text is referred to as a myth, it is clear what is being stated. When dealing with a myth, especially one that a faith community is holding as a "revealed" myth, we are dealing with a text in which a sacred truth is being told. We are dealing with the communication of a community's understanding of itself in relation to God, the larger world, indeed salvation history. We are hearing the conveyance of a particular community's deepest meanings and symbols.

Stating that a narrative is a myth is in no way making a claim about the statement's ability or inability to convey a truth. The difference is merely one of methodology. This difference between myth and modern post-Enlightenment propositional claims has been evocatively brought forth in a modern piece of literature by Yann Martel entitled *Life of Pi*, in which the author sets this very issue as the basis of his gripping novel by having the story relayed one way (as a highly metaphorical and symbolic rendering) and then at the very end reinterpreted into the other (a modern rendering).

Martel's ingenious narrative begins with a young Indian boy's journey to Canada with his family on a ship. Midway through the voyage, the boat sinks and the boy finds himself alone in a small dingy with a group of wild animals. As they drift slowly, alone in the baking sun, the animals begin to revert to their instinctual patterns. The small boy fends off their advances as best he can but watches in horror as they commence in demonstrating survival of the fittest. After much travail, the boy is found. The boy is cared for, and when his strength is returned, his Japanese rescuers interrogate him endlessly until he finally lets go of the account he has repeated faithfully over and over and reframes it for them, resentfully. Each animal becomes a person. Each event stays as it was, but now no longer is the death struggle between the tiger and the orangutan, rather it was between a terrorist and his mother. In the end, the reader is left to ask which version of the story is "true." Or are both true? If so, which is richer, more horrific, and more real?

So this journey begins. It is not meant to be a journey of mere ideas. It is a call for us to wake up and to remember who we are and what we have been called to be. It is a call to each of us to reclaim our humanity, to accept our radical freedom and the associated responsibility and accountability, not just for ourselves but also for our children, neighbors, communities, and people of God everywhere. It all begins with life. The New Testament (John 10:10) quotes Jesus of Nazareth as having said, "I came that you might have life and have it more abundantly." If there is one major objective to this work, it is the same: that in writing this and in reading this we both may choose life and in so doing have it in abundance—not just for ourselves, but for all those we touch each and every day.

Understanding Humanity Through the Creation Myths of the Old Testament

To understand yourself as a Christian, you must first understand yourself as a human being. That understanding requires each of us to stand back from the day-to-day happenings associated with the living of our lives so that we can see who we are and question ourselves about the meaning—or potential lack of meaning—that characterizes the selves we have become. It requires that we allow ourselves to ask what our lives are about or maybe what they should be about. It often entails pondering the nature of what it means to be human regardless of race, color, and creed. It can include such musings as do we see ourselves as merely one of a multitude of species that come into being and disappear? Or perhaps does each of us have a meaningful role in a larger context that we may not fully comprehend? Or could it be that we, like every other creature, merely exist, procreate, and pass on the collective wisdom and genetic makeup of our species to yet another generation and then die? Understanding what we really believe it means to be a human being, what powers we are blessed with, what limitations we may have, and their potential effects on who we are and who we may become, as well as our effects on others, is critical in understanding ourselves, our relationships, and society in general.

Whether one perceives oneself as an actor in one's own life or as a victim of circumstances beyond one's control has significant implications for how one lives. Is one disposition or the other more justified? Who each of us is and becomes is in great part the result of how each perceives himself or herself in his or her world. Are we victims of fate or circumstances? Do we have control, and are we free and thus responsible for our freedom? Is this life what we make of it? Is it absurd? Is it a gift of great worth or hell itself? Is it a test, and am I being watched and graded? Are we different than the other creatures with which we share this earth? Is there more to our lives than just the act of living? Where one stands on this continuum of possible views is the starting point of identifying the context of a common notion of humanity.

Where does one begin to formulate a rational view of who we are as human beings and how our limitations and possibilities factor into our identities? This is a central question in coming to terms with ourselves. For our purposes, the ancient Jewish myths of creation will be used as our point of departure in addressing many of these questions. What truths about humanity are layered in their multi-textured images? Are there possibly any insights we might gain about who we are, who we might be, as well as why we are, from their ancient wisdom? As most scholars admit, many of these creation myths are not purely Jewish in their origin but the amalgamation of creation stories of the various people of the period and the locale. In fact, many of the key features found in both the Genesis creation myths are found in other coexistent creation myths of peoples of the same time and place.

The question of why we exist was posed by the Baltimore Catechism, which was used to instruct neophytes in the Roman Catholic faith about the basic foundations concerning humanity, God, and their relationship. This primacy in determining the potential purpose of human existence through asking the basic question of why we were created forced a natural linkage between God's purpose in creating us and our purpose as created beings into clear relief. The methodology of this catechism was quite simple. A question was raised, and then the answer was given. This allowed an exhaustive list of topics to be systematically and logically dealt with much in the same way one would progress in learning geometry. For each question and its answer were ordered such that a systematic theology could be constructed by starting with the simpler components and progressing to the more complex. The first question offered was why was humanity created in the first place? The answer proffered was that God created humanity to know and to love him. Though the answer is apparently simple, it would take many of the children who learned it by rote years to grasp its meaning and subtlety.

The Old Testament itself addressed this same theme in one of the creation myths of Genesis. (There are two separate creation myths in Genesis.) The myth tells of the first man, Adam, and his wife, Eve, and their pristine existence in the garden of paradise. For in this myth, God created all the creatures as well as a man (the meaning of Adam in Hebrew) and woman, Eve. He placed them in the garden of paradise, called Eden. Paradise was completely different than our world. God walked freely among his creatures in Eden (Genesis 3:8). There was no evil, pain, or toil. Adam and Eve had no need for clothing, for they had no impure thoughts, no shame. They lived there with all the creatures that God had created in perfect bliss. When one considers the kind of place this paradise was, it certainly has many fine attributes: no sickness, suffering, or death. The question that needs to be considered before we proceed is, do the Adam and Eve of paradise significantly resemble humanity as we experience it today? Certainly, Adam and Eve are God's creation of the first man and the first woman, but are they human beings in any way one would consider the term as applied to our species today? In order to answer this question, we need to continue with our description of paradise and the story that unfolds.

At the center of paradise or the garden, God placed a special tree called the tree of the knowledge of good and evil. Adam and Eve were told that they could eat of all the various fruit-bearing trees and bushes that filled paradise, but they were to neither touch nor eat (Genesis 2:16; Genesis 3:2–4) of the fruit of this tree at its center or they would die. God not only created this specific tree with its enticing fruit, he placed it right in the center of the garden. God also sent into the garden the serpent whose sole purpose was to ensure that Eve could be properly tempted to disobey God's explicit command. Through the snake, God made sure that both Adam and Eve understood that this tree and its fruit had a certain power, i.e., to bestow the ability to know the difference between good and evil and thus the ability to choose between them (Genesis 3:5). It appears that this was the only restriction that was given to either Adam or Eve or any other creature. Clearly, up to this juncture in the myth, we have Adam and Eve, childlike creatures capable of living and filling their needs in a perfect environment with no consequences. God can be among them and can enjoy his creation, but to say that God could be loved by these first humans would be to seriously mangle its meaning. As we shall emphasize throughout, the concept of love as a programmed response for which there is no other possible alternative may be affection but hardly love.

As most of us are aware, Eve was tempted by the serpent and ate the fruit of the Tree of the Knowledge of Good and Evil and then gave the fruit to Adam to eat, which led to their expulsion from paradise. This is not, however, where we want to dwell for our particular purposes. Where we want to focus first is on what this myth is telling us about who we are and the nature of our relationship to God. The particular interpretation of the core meaning of this text is the belief that God wanted humanity both to know and love him and second, that God wanted his creature to have the "knowledge of good and evil," i.e. choice as a necessary prerequisite.

This may appear unorthodox at first blush. This interpretation is meant to evoke potentially new insights into our understandings of ourselves as human beings and of God. In the narrative, Eve's eating of the fruit of this tree created an irreparable rift between paradise and humanity, but it is important to note that this separation was not between God and humanity. This point is not often focused on in commentaries concerned with this text. However, it is an important distinction. The eating of the forbidden fruit made it so that Adam and Eve could no longer live in Eden. It did not separate them from their Creator. It did not cause God to wipe them and all of creation from existence. It did not cause God to send a flood as he would later on after Noah had finished his ark in an attempt to start again. In fact, this act of Eve's disobedience would set up the possibility of a new relationship between the Creator and the creature. It made possible for the first time a relationship of choice between creature and Creator, man and woman, as well as all of the creatures that would now exist in a new context.

Later in history, this relationship of choice between God and humanity would develop into a more refined model characterized by covenant, the mutual agreement of two parties to bind themselves to each other in mutual devotion. This notion of covenant was to be the very nexus of the relationship between God and his people of Israel. This relationship between God and humanity would grow as humanity grew in self-understanding and would reach a completely new representation in the chosen people, who were to become the children of Abraham.

These children of Abraham were selected as God's chosen people as a result of Abraham's demonstrated love, his choice. Abraham was asked to sacrifice his only son as a sign of his singular devotion and fidelity to God. Abraham's choice, his act of will to offer Isaac, demonstrated this love, his unfettered faith in his God, which became the foundation of the creation of an unparalleled love story between God and Israel (Genesis 22). It also became the very model upon which this same God, according to Christian believers, would later replay this act—this time inverting the demonstration as God now offered his son in sacrifice as the demonstration of his love for his creation. In both of these cases, the love that is expressed by the creature for the Creator and the Creator for the creature pivots on the ability of humanity to choose other than as God would will them. This basic capacity for knowing what is right and what is wrong and having the capacity to make that choice freely and without external interference is certainly a prerequisite to the capacity to love that each of these stories profoundly demonstrates.

As we know, God spared Isaac and stayed Abraham's knife-wielding hand as an act of mercy. "You do not delight in burnt offering" (Psalm 51:16). God's objective was to know if Abraham loved him with all his heart. God, in the gift of his son, did not stay his hand in offering Jesus as his perfect and unparalleled expression of love for us. However, "No greater love has man than to lay down his life for his friends" (John 15:13). In both cases, however, the ability of Abraham and Jesus to choose a different path is essential in order to appreciate the gift each was willing to make as the expression of their singular and profound love of the God they worshiped.

God chose to create humanity in order that we might know and love him. Equally as important, God desired humanity's love. This desire to be loved by humanity is what links these two seemingly disassociated points, the statement from the Baltimore Catechism and the Adam and Eve myth. For only through our ability to know good and evil and thus to be able to choose as an act of individual will, freely expressed, could God ever achieve his desired outcome of love from mankind.

God's desire for humanity's love was formally expressed in the

Great Commandment offered by Jesus, which summarized the first three of the Ten Commandments, as well as the spirit of the social aspects of the six negative commandments: "Thou shall love the Lord thy God with all thy heart, and with all thy soul, and with all thy mind, and with all thy strength. This is the first commandment. And the second is like, namely this; Thou shall love thy neighbor as thyself. There is none other commandment greater than these" (Mark 13:30). God's desire to be loved is cemented in the first commandment as the very heart of both Judaic law and later as the declared proper orientation of a Christian's entire worldview. Here the Great Commandment couples the love of God, which remains primary, with the love of neighbor in an inextricable manner. Here the love of God is carried forward from the old covenant to the new as the centerpiece of the good news of this new expression of the Jewish faith. It is the same love that required Adam and Eve to be able to do other than what was prescribed in paradise. For Adam and Eve to become completely human, they had to have the capacity to will freely. They had to be able to choose to love their Creator or not. For without this capacity to choose, Adam and Eve were not significantly different than God's other creatures, whose natures dictated their behavior and therefore from whom God could not expect love and upon whom God could not place responsibility or accountability.

Another piece of the Old Testament concerning the nature of the human creature also occurs in the Genesis creation myths. This section adds increasing depth to the nature of the free will that Adam and Eve were granted in the sweet taste of the fruit of the tree that offered the knowledge of good and evil, the fruit that Milton would postulate as the delectable apple in *Paradise Lost*. It adds clarity to the continued Genesis myth by placing this new capacity of humanity within the construct of humanity's participation in the individual creation of each person. When God decided to create humanity, it is said in the Vulgate Bible that he created them *ad imago Dei*, that is, "to or toward the image of God." This is not how we usually see it translated, but this literal translation of the Latin encapsulates significant meaning and nuance, which adds to our understanding of our natures and potential.

The importance of this translation to the understanding of ourselves is that humanity is not created "in" the image of God. That is, we are not an image as a given. Humanity can become an image of God, that is, we were created with the potential to be images of God. This idea of *theosis* lies at the heart of Orthodox Christianity. We were not, however, programmed as images of God. From this perspective, the continued role of the human will, i.e. our ability to choose freely, is placed as the crux of humanity's opportunity. God designed humanity with the inclination that we should be like him, but he did not demand it. In fact, he gave us a piece of his own power by making us "little less than the angels" (Psalm 8:6). That piece of himself is our ability to will, i.e., to freely choose. It is the ability to choose not to love God as well as it is the ability to choose to love God; to choose not to be like God as much as to choose to be like God; to choose not to become his image as each of us were uniquely created to be, or to choose to become the very image that he created for each of us, which is his very image.

From what has been revealed thus far, we know that we have been created with a capacity to be free, free first to love God and then our neighbors. A very specific connection has been established between this capacity to love and our ability to freely choose, the ability to exercise our will. In fact, a fundamental premise of this work is that love is fundamentally an act of the will. It is love, as an act of the will, which makes it possible for us to will ourselves to fulfill the image that God created us as capable of achieving. If, therefore, one's stated love is not a free act of one's will, one cannot be speaking about love. The question that must then be raised and answered is what specifically the human is willing in the act of loving and what the role of feeling and emotions are in our act of love.

Humanity's freedom and ability to will, to act, are the primary methods of self-creation and discovery that will be the foundation of the concept of humanity necessary as the bedrock for the reality of the Christian disciple.

The Adam and Eve myth clearly establishes that God's desire to empower his creature with the capacity to choose to love him or not was a fundamental presupposition of God's creative act. It is also central to appreciating the gift of his son as our Redeemer, as well as humanity's vocation to participate in the redemption that was begun by Jesus, but only possessed through the exercise of will in response to this calling. God did not want paradise defined by programmed humans incapable of making mistakes. For paradise was a place devoid of the kind of being God desired, a being that could not will in any meaningful sense.

Prior to the expulsion within the Genesis narrative context, it would be strange to even think of Adam and Eve as full persons as we are persons. They were, in many respects, more aligned with the other creatures that populated Eden. Choice, in the sense of real options, would have been foreign to both Adam and Eve. When they were hungry, they ate. When they had any other biological need, they responded to it. Eating this or that certainly was a possible option, but not in the sense of a willed choice requiring real outcomes and associated accountability and responsibility. It was paradise in every sense of the word. In fact, the idea of a choice of the kind that followed their expulsion had to be introduced within the myth context by an outsider, the snake.

There is, however, a message buried deep within this myth. For instance, why does God place this tree in the garden in the first place? Why does God make this tree explicitly off limits? Why is it in the center of the garden? The myth does not say, but its unfolding makes it apparent that these things were done to achieve a specific outcome. God desired Adam and Eve's freedom, their knowledge of good and evil, which was made possible in the creation of the object of temptation for the snake to use. God wanted a world with choice. He wanted a creature with a will, a will that would involve real choices with profound consequences. The most profound consequence of his creature having a will would be his or her having the ability to love him or his or her having the ability to turn away from him. Specifically, he desired a creature with a will to love.

This presupposition meant that God had to be willing to create a world for humanity and all creatures in which acts of will would make sense. This requires a world in which real choices yield real outcomes. It requires a world in which men and women could rationally understand and foresee these outcomes, even if only with a degree of accuracy and probability. A world in which creatures could exercise their wills and make decisions is a world filled with paradoxes. It is a world of laws that structure how things work and interact. It is a world of cause and effect, physics and science. At the same time, as will be argued, it is a world in which human beings must have freedom and wills that can express that freedom. This world would thus be humanity's sphere.

God's power to intercede in humanity's world, by his choice, had to be subject to the primacy of his desire for humans to have real wills and thus a world in which these wills would make sense. This meant that God needed to decide if he was willing to allow this world to operate in such a manner as to make human will and human freedom possible. This entailed that God had to be willing to limit his own power to intervene in this world and arbitrarily alter the natural unfolding of the world with its natural laws as well as humanity and its ability to act. For if God were to arbitrarily interject, correct, or alter reality, then responsibility, accountability, and the subsequent outcomes, even those that are not intentional but are the natural conclusion of many forgotten actions, would be suspect. Where there are not predictable outcomes, responsibility, and accountability, there cannot be freedom or will. Without the weight of the knowledge that our choices will have implications for which we are responsible, the concepts of will and freedom become meaningless. God thus created an environment in which his interventions would be seriously self-limited in order that the love he sought could be possible.

This in no way is positing a Deistic God who made his watch, wound it, and then sat back and let things unfold as they would. This is a God who created this situation in order that he might be loved. This is an empathic and personal God who imbued into his creature the capacity to be his arms and legs, his voice and to participate in the ultimate redemption of all creation. Deism is a theory of a deity who created and then was no more, in the sense of involvement. The God being described above is in love with this creature humanity and, as an expression of this love, has freely stayed his hand.

The creation myth presented above demands freedom as a necessary prerequisite for the desired love sought by the Creator. God's gift of freedom not only gave agency to each person but also fundamentally shaped the remainder of creation. The world in which humanity lives, along with the creatures that share this world, is part of a set of natural processes and laws that continue to unfold both within and around humanity. Some of these occurrences are part of what we call nature. These events have causes and outcomes. Some of these outcomes can be horrible and wreak massive destruction and death. The laws that control nature are not, as the ancients believed, the outcomes of all too humanlike gods, but non-moral laws (laws of nature). These laws are non-moral in that no one is specifically to blame. They are the result of the actual playing out of a myriad of causes and their subsequent effects. Nature is responsible for incredible wonders and possibilities for creation, as well as horrible catastrophes and challenges such as plagues and natural disasters. Added to these natural forces are humanity's actions, which, while discrete, are part of the complex interwoven network of actions and reactions, causes and effects, which over time can be difficult to separate into neat groups. It is for this reason that the lines between moral and non-moral actions can become quite blurred.

God created a world in which he chose to let his creatures' will be exercised for its good and for its detriment. He chose to create a world in which the will of his creatures would yield real results, not just for each person in each moment, but in aggregate, like waves over time. The sum total of these choices over time would yield unforeseen outcomes for generations yet to be born. The accumulations of each of our choices as individuals and as communities, which are a conglomeration of good and bad decisions, weave together as history progresses and do not just yield specific outcomes tied to specific choices. Our choices unfold into unforeseen and unfathomed consequences for all future generations.

Based on the mythology of the Old Testament, God, therefore, by his own design, chose to allow humanity's world to unfold according to the ordered laws of cause and effect within every human experience. God restrained his ability to directly and invasively intercede in the natural order of the created world as a necessary prerequisite for the possibility of human free will. This restraint is critical to appreciate as the prerequisite of freedom, which demands real outcomes resulting from freely engaged wills. The ability to choose without the notion of predictable outcomes is no freedom at all. Choosing to jump out a window on the twenty-fourth floor is not a real choice if the consequences are purely random or nonexistent. Real freedom is predicated upon the reality of a bone-crushing landing. By no means does every act of humanity have a guaranteed outcome. This would be absurd, but one of many probable outcomes does follow our actions. When I get up in the morning, I have no fear that, when I put my feet to the floor, the floor will just open up and swallow me. The inability to predict the exact outcome of our actions does not mitigate the fact that our actions do have predictable outcomes, but sometimes we may not have considered the ones we receive.

There are obvious implications of the position we have proposed in which God restrains his ability to intrude in this world to accommodate a free creature. Understanding the numerous accounts of God's apparent interventions within the Old and New Testaments must now be considered in light of the above proposition. For both the Old and New Testaments abound in stories of God's seeming intervention into this world. This apparent inconsistency must be resolved both to accommodate the rich biblical tradition and to make space for the ongoing intense care and wooing of humanity that is part and parcel of the Judeo-Christian experience of God.

Holistic anthropology and theology does not need to diminish belief in an intimate, caring God as a logical outcome. The position that God refrains from intervening directly does not entail that we do not have a God who suffers the burdens of our moral choices or the world's non-moral outcomes, as made manifest in nature's beauty and fury. The belief stance being taken is that God chose to create a universe in which there existed a creature, the human being, for which he desired the capacity to will to love him and thus required a world suitable to that purpose.

This world of natural laws and predictable consequences is not, however, beyond God's ongoing involvement. The nexus where the divine will and the human will converge is in humanity's capacity to be open to God's call and to invite God to work in and through us as his emissaries here on earth. This has been the role of the prophets, the saints, and indeed even the Son himself. It is the singular challenge of the faithful to, through free will, hear his call and to follow him in freedom. This aligning of wills and following the commands God asks of us is what makes his presence apparent.

Delving into the specifics of what this means for us in understanding ourselves, our position in this world, and our understanding of our relationship to God is critical to a complete picture of the human person and the call of Christianity built upon it. Reflecting upon the true nature of freedom will also evoke greater clarity about the nature of the relationship between this God for whom love is so central and the creature, who seems so alone and vulnerable in this world crafted to enable his/her ability to will that love.

Freedom as the Seed of Being Human

The worldview and the concept of humanity presented thus far have created an apparent paradox between creation, imbued with immutable laws as the basis for the possibility of human freedom, and the very radical freedom that is being postulated and expressed through humanity's capacity to will. How can humanity be free in a world ruled by cause and effect? Isn't freedom merely humanity's ignorance of causes? There is no paradox; rather creation with its rational constructs, cause-effect, and action-reaction is a necessary precursor to freedom. How can this make sense? It is somewhat easier to see how the laws of creation are necessary as a foundation to freedom than to answer the question of how you can have freedom in a world driven by such rigid laws. Certainly one can accept that freedom without consequence, responsibility, or accountability at any level is counterintuitive. Freedom must, by its nature, include choice, and the choice must include outcomes, consequences. These consequences must to some degree be predictable. If they are not in any way predictable (within the limits of probability, nuance, and error) then the idea of a meaningful act of the individual will is not clear and is possibly counterintuitive.

At first blush, it would appear that we have boxed ourselves into a very tight corner. It has been admitted that the world in which humanity lives is governed by very strict rules of cause and effect. It has been unequivocally stated that no distinctions can be drawn between humans as members of this ecosphere and the ecosphere itself. Humanity cannot be perceived as merely pins stuck in this globe. We are pieces of the created fabric just as rocks, birds, trees, fish, etc. are. Where, then, can one find space for this radical freedom or for the true acts of will not governed by the very laws of the beings that we are?

Many modern philosophers would point out that, from the first moment of our arrival on this earth, each person appears to have been robbed of any potential for freedom, for none of us was consulted in this radical choice to be born. Every day, one can read or hear about how much of what happens to our bodies and even our personalities are purported to be either directly or indirectly attributable to a genome or the unique DNA pattern that one inherited. How many times has one heard about a tragic accident occurring as the result of someone being at the wrong place at the wrong time? How many times has the complaint been leveled against someone when something positive happens because of no particular merit of his or her own, rather because of whom they know or the fact that they happened to be in the right place at the right time? So much of our experience seems to be telling us that we are not responsible because we are not free; our actions are not the result of our wills.

What makes this so frightening is that as a culture we seem to vacillate between wanting to believe that we are free and should be accountable, and desperately wanting to flee from this freedom and its looming accountability. Our culture has mastered the "I was not responsible because" defense. One of the most notorious examples of this was the San Francisco "Twinkie" defense used in the Milk murder, in which it was argued that the murderer of two San Francisco political leaders was not something for which the accused should have been held culpable due to the influence of a recently eaten Twinkie. This argument, which was supported by the testimony of a psychiatrist, actually enabled the accused to receive reduced charges. The real question is how humanity is free and thus how humanity is accountable. Without answering this in a meaningful way, we have neither the tools to understand our potential, our power, nor an ability to understand how to hold ourselves or each other accountable or for what. As a result, questions of culpability, which are even more subtle, are open for all kinds of potential distortions. From a spiritual perspective, the entire notion of our Christian call to be both witnesses to the truth of Christ's message and to bring God's kingdom to this earth can have no real meaning without freedom and accountability.

It should be apparent from what has preceded that the concept of freedom is anything but simple. Certainly freedom has been a key concern of human history. People have written about and fought for their freedom personally, as societies, and as nation-states. Our freedoms of speech, religion, to bear arms, to congregate, *habeas corpus,* and due process, while often central to discussions concerning freedom, are not our particular focus. These are but a few of the freedoms for which humans have shown themselves willing to shed their blood. While these broad notions of freedom are certainly important, it is not these particular aspects of freedom that need attention to further the understanding of ourselves and our role in this world. In order to clarify the aspect of freedom that is central to our understanding of being human and being called to be co-redeemers of this world, a distinction is required between two frequently misused and misunderstood terms: freedom and liberty.

Certainly, our ability to choose external events is not always completely within our power. My having been born in the middle of the twentieth century was never my choice. My having contracted appendicitis at eight was not my doing, either. As most of us did not choose our coming into this world or its particular circumstances, neither will most of us choose the day or manner by which we leave this world. A significant number of key aspects of our lives, capabilities, and circumstances have not been ours to determine, yet our claim is that we are not only free, but we are radically so. How can both of these positions be held simultaneously? If the will has as its object the ability to choose among externals, then this is not genuine human freedom, but liberty. If the will is focused on the meanings we give to external realities, then this is genuine human freedom. Thus the essence of freedom is the object the will is focused upon.

By distinguishing between these two alternative objects, it should become clear where the most complete exercise of our wills is possible and where we must acknowledge very real existential constraints. It is through reflecting upon the distinction between these two very different realities, liberty and freedom, that each of us will be given the opportunity to better understand the complexities of our natures as potential images of the divine and how and with what tools we can achieve this most serious mission. We should also become more specifically aware of where and how we are responsible and thus accountable to ourselves, to our neighbors, and to our Creator. We will also elucidate where culpability needs to be tempered by an appreciation of the constraints with which each of us will battle as part of life.

Gaining clarity about human freedom is best begun by first differentiating between it and liberty. Liberty is our ability to make choices among externals. Examples of what is meant by externals include the choice between two pieces of chocolate or the decision to take this road versus that. The external choices humans are confronted with range from the sublime to the ridiculous, from the choice of which college to attend to the socks I put on in the morning.

External choices are always constrained. Some of these constraints can be biological. I may have certain limitations in my physical makeup that limit my ability to play pro ball or to be a concert musician. Some constraints can be economical, social, psychological, or innumerable other limiting factors. In some cases, these constraints can be so obvious that, no matter how serious the outcome of a specific choice by an individual, we as a society have recognized in law that any culpability associated with that choice must be mitigated. Liberty is thus always constrained.

Human history is awash with stories of humanity's attempt to gain and maintain the liberties that each of us as children of God has an equal right to. Even today, marginalized members of societies are fighting for their rights all over the globe. Liberties are important and worthy of our diligent protection, but liberty should never be confused with freedom. Liberty is the ability to be unencumbered by unnecessary external forces in the making of personal choices about such things as where one can live, what religion one can practice, where one can go to school, and with whom one can associate, as well as many more vital questions. While our liberties may be taken from us, our freedom can never be compromised by another human being. Each of us has internal constraints that bind our liberty, such as physical and mental capacities. Each of us has situational constraints into which we have been born, such as our economic resources, the nature of the families we have been born into, as well as the constraints of our times and cultures. No government or society can give or take your freedom, but they can severely constrain and/or expand your liberties.

Liberty, defined as the ability to choose externals, is certainly a part of what we mean when we use the word freedom. Unfortunately, the confusion between these two important concepts has led many to forget what real freedom is and where it lies. Liberty is not the most essential aspect of our freedom. Liberty is our ability to manipulate things through personal power, money, or charisma. For the affluent, powerful, or charismatic, this confusion between liberties and true freedom can sometimes appear all too real. The space created by affluence and power can give the illusion that the will's proper orientation is to fill that void with things, activities, travel, memberships, and connections. Affluence and influence and what these can procure and manipulate can provide an illusion of the will's ability to control what is ultimately uncontrollable. This distortion can misdirect the will and seem to invest human beings with more capacity than they actually have. The affluent often believe they can control reality and that those held dear can be made safe from life's unfolding mystery through their ample means and influence.

This illusion is not just a temptation for individuals but also for societies as a whole. The consequences for those who fall victim to this delusion can be devastating. Life will inevitably correct this fiction, and the winds of fate will expose the delusion that humans can control very much at all when it comes to externals. It is also a serious question as to the proper amount of liberty that any individual or society should have. Just because I can does not answer the harder question of whether I should. Liberty as the optimal minimizing of external constraints on an individual's or a society's or a nation-state's will is a source of serious concern and dialogue. It would be a serious mistake to assume that unfettered will at any level is optimal. In fact, a completely unfettered will that expresses itself without a proper grounding can be more expressive of the demonic than of the divine.

The question that now remains is what is the essence of freedom? Our ability to make external choices is certainly an aspect of freedom, but it is clearly not the essence. The role of the human will has been demonstrated to be central to human liberty, and its link to freedom is obvious. So while the human will is a necessary condition for freedom, we now know it is not a sufficient condition. The secret to discovering the essence of human freedom requires us to focus not on the human capacity to will, but rather on the object of the act of willing. Discovering that unfettered fulfillment of our wishes is not an adequate definition of freedom opens up the whole question of who we are and what the purpose to life is, if there is one.

True freedom is not constrained as is liberty. Freedom is the predecessor of our external actions and choices and thus the reason for its stated primacy. It is our capacity to give meaning to the events of our lives. It enables one to choose the basic meaning that one gives to who one is and one's place in this world. It underlies the reflexive manner in which I experience myself and others that is unique to each individual's existence as well as each individual's relationship to the world (people, places, things). It is a pre-experiential posture that establishes my conscious "in the moment" experience of myself as a unique individual. It is the filter through which I experience myself as past and project myself as existing into the next moment (future). It is the context through which I perceive reality, and thus, the position from which reality is constituted.

This definition of freedom as the ability for humans to fundamentally contribute to what may naively appear as an objective external reality by acknowledging that each of us has the capacity to determine if and how an external event will be internalized by the meanings that I can and will give it. Freedom, unlike liberty, is unconstrained by the externals. The more one becomes aware of this fundamental capacity to transcend the events and situations that life can and will present us with, the more we have the capacity to transcend these events as pure givens.

Grasping this powerful reality that we can significantly alter our lives and who we are through greater control of our wills and how we choose to experience ourselves and the events that confront us through the meanings we choose is not an easy task. Many of us will take years to master our emotions and our fears so that we can come to exercise this facet of our beings. For some of us, there will always be areas where exercising our freedom will be very challenging. While it may seem glib to say that we have this capacity and that it is an essential aspect of our beings, it would be a terrible misapprehension to think that this capacity or power is always easy to exercise. Like any capacity we have that we wish to master, we must practice and develop the natural inclination into a honed skill. Our wills and our ability to use this capacity is no exception. Freedom is thus ours as a natural facet of our beings, but this does not mean its proper exercise is always intuitive and easy.

Whether one raises the meanings of events or even of one's very self to a conscious level is the first and primary issue. For the meanings we may give to any event or to our lives as a whole are the true objects of our wills. This means that while one may experience one's liberties as ways in which one exercises one's personal will, this is an illusion with potentially grave consequence. There is a significant difference between a life lived mainly through reactions and a life lived through chosen responses. Each individual as a unique person is more the result of the meanings chosen by him or her than of the things that happen to him/her. In short, I am certainly partly constituted by experiences, but most significantly I am my chosen meanings, which I give to the key experiences of my life.

The world in which each of us lives, the things that happen to us and that we do in life, are all secondary. What is primary to understanding who I am and to knowing the world I live in are the outcomes of my unique and specific capacity to give meanings to what I perceive, not the perceptions themselves. Anyone living at the level of reaction will live a life that will buffet him or her one way then another. He will experience himself as a victim of fate, both good and bad, and will find himself constantly trying to find the link between events and justice in life. The difference is that the person enlightened in the knowledge of where her freedom truly resides is open to an entirely new way of existing, perceiving, and responding. This pinpointing of what freedom really is and what it involves is merely the beginning of unfolding the related aspects of our existence.

A critical complement to this aspect of ourselves as free—as co-creators of our individual identities and the world—is expressive of our natures as symbol makers. It is as symbol makers that we discover the foundation of our ability to both express ourselves and communicate with our world. It is the mechanism through which we express who we are and what our internal experiences are. Humanity uses language, gesture, ritual, and images as the bridges between our internal selves and the external world with which we interact. These are symbols which do more than just communicate oneself to others, for they are the methods whereby an individual creates him or herself as well.

Humanity's symbolic capacity is what has allowed it to transcend the natural instincts and drives that totally control the remainder of the animal kingdom. It is this distancing from instinct and our ability to choose and create ourselves and our world through symbols that is at the core of the unique essence of the human person. One might argue that high-level mammals other than human beings can create symbols and this may indeed be true, but not to the extent to which humans do. It is important to note that symbols, which by definition are external expressions that point to or give utterance to internal realities, are therefore inherently social in nature. Symbols are the methods we use to share our internal feelings, thoughts, and emotions with another. Language is an example of a critical symbol for humans.

My dog, Harry, can enable us to reflect on some of the basic differences between many of the other creatures that humanity interacts with and us. Harry exists in a fundamentally different way than we do. Not only is Harry less encumbered by the issues of meaning, but he is also not imbued with the full capacity to symbolically interact with the world in language, images, gestures, and rituals. As a human being, I both use and create symbols to express my ideas, my happiness at winning a contest or the quiet awe associated with a profound experience. These symbols are imbued with meanings, and they express my interpretations of the world. These symbols can expose a set of life orientations committed to alleviating pain and suffering as the externalization of hope, faith, and wonder that inform my worldview. While human beings can transcend the suffering that each of us will endure, it would be a mistake to think that this means we can get rid of our personal suffering. The human capacity to choose the meaning of the pleasurable and painful aspects of life must inform how I choose to make sense of the vicissitudes of existence.

All of the complex thoughts, ideas, words, images, and the meanings that symbols expose open infinite possibility, opportunity, and hope that are the inherent potentials within each person. This is the undetermined creative locus in which the human will operates as co-creator of the unfinished self and the world in which it will choose to live. This is the sacred core from which each individual can and must operate. While it may aid us in accepting something painful by allowing us to understand it within a broader set of meanings, it will not take our pain away. Having to endure a terrible loss is and always will be a difficult and a heart-rending aspect of life, but the experience of this loss as stupid, unnecessary, and meaningless is quite different. How the individual faced with this trauma internalizes the events through their ability to choose a set of meanings will be at the core of both how they experience this trauma and what they are able to learn from it.

Through the proper use of the will, we have discovered what will be the key for achieving our personal salvation and the redemption of our world. Up to now, we have described freedom and the human will as the creators of a space from which humanity is empowered to make choices first and foremost concerning the self each will choose to be and then of the families, communities, and world they will collectively choose to inhabit. It is meaning that both constructs the world we each encounter and informs our actions. A person who sees life and his own struggles as futile and absurd is not just constructing a self that will interpret his experiences through this filter; he is also laying the foundation for the actions that will flow from this view of the world and his specific place in it. How each of us interprets the actions and choices of others flows from the fundamental meanings that permeate our very way of being in the world. This cycle of meaning, interpretation, and action, if not challenged, will continue to infect others by creating the very world this chosen posture expects. It is for this reason that conversion, both at a human level and at a spiritual level, requires being struck down and blinded like St. Paul, so that once the scales of hopelessness, fear, anger, and cynicism are challenged there is the space to determine what and how we internalize our lives and the experiences we encounter in everyday living.

Human beings have many options when choosing the core (the space in which our meanings operate) from which they will establish their identities, their worldviews. This core is the central meaning that establishes a person's fundamental frame of reference. Some people live from a core based on inferiority or lack of self-esteem. This can lead to a worldview infused with constant assessments of where one stands in relationship to others. It can be the source of a life prone to envy, bitterness, fear, competitiveness, and manipulation. Some people live with a fundamental core focused on power or its handmaiden, money. This orientation can lead to persons with tendencies to attempt to control and use other people as a means to their desired end. It is no wonder that Jesus stated, "I tell you the truth, it is hard for a rich man to enter the kingdom of heaven. Again I tell you, it is easier for a camel to go through the eye of a needle than for a rich man to enter the kingdom of God" (Matthew 19:24). It is essential to note that the message here is not just the trivial concern for money, but more importantly, a concern for those of us who believe we have enough. It is a warning against being satisfied with ourselves and the temptation to draw very clear limits around our lives. It is a warning against being complete in this life, wherein our souls cease to be as the Psalmist described "As the deer pants for the water brooks, so pants my soul for You, O God. My soul thirsts for God, for the living God. When shall I come and appear before God?" (Psalm 42:1–2). Our right orientation must be one of incompleteness and hope-filled expectancy. By incompleteness, I am thinking of a glass half filled and thus capable of receiving more of the rich and limitless abundance that is ours if we have but the courage and humility. In this poem by George Herbert, this concept is most beautifully espoused.

When God at first made man,
Having a glass of blessings standing by;
Let us (said he) pour on him all we can:
Let the world's riches, which dispersed lie,
    Contract into a span.
So strength first made a way;
The beauty flow'd, then wisdom, honor, pleasure:
When almost all was out, God made a stay,
Perceiving that lone of all his treasure
    Rest in the bottom lay.
For if I should (said he)
Bestow this jewel also on my creature,
He would adore my gifts instead of me,
And rest in Nature, not the God of Nature:
    So both should losers be.
Yet let him keep the rest,
But keep them with repining restlessness:
Let him be rich and weary, that at least,
If goodness lead him not, yet weariness
    May toss him to my breast.

—George Herbert
(1593–1633)

Satisfaction and satiation are not the dispositions that lead to the growth of a Christian soul. Nor is the avaricious pursuit of things—power, money, and fame—the rightful occupation of our wills. In a world that adores those who possess these things, we must consistently ask ourselves what this adoration means. "For what will it profit a man if he gains the whole world and forfeits his life? For the Son of man has come with his angels in the glory of his Father, and then he will repay every man for what he has done" (Matthew 16:26–27). In the poetry of the metaphysical poet John Donne, this appreciation for the tempering of the soul via the suffering of our lives brings us to the intimate embrace of the ineffable source of our beings.

Batter My Heart, Three-Person'd God

Batter my heart, three person'd God; for, you
As yet but knocke, breathe, shine, and seeke to mend;
That I may rise, and stand, o'erthrow mee,'and bend
Your force, to breake, blow, burn and make me new.
    I, like an usurpt towne, to'another due,
Labour to'admit you, but Oh, to no end,
Reason your viceroy in mee, mee should defend,
But is captiv'd, and proves weake or untrue.
Yet dearley'I love you,'and would be loved faine,
    But am betroth'd unto your enemie:
Divorce mee,'untie, or breake that knot againe,
Take mee to you, imprison mee, for I
Except you'enthrall mee, never shall be free,
Nor ever chast, except you ravish mee.
          —John Donne (1572–1631)

Not all the options must be negative, however. A principle-centered person frames his sense of himself and others through acts of conscious will, which choose values and principles that act as both his or her source and vitality. As Christians, we declare that we will live a principle-centered life founded on the basic Judeo-Christian values espoused by Jesus and the prophets. Examples of these life-centered principles are faith, hope, and love, which have been called the theological virtues. Other Christian principles are generosity of spirit, joy, humility, and forgiveness, as well as inclusivity and refraining from judgment. Accepting the inherent mystery and giftedness of life, not just in externals but also in my very self, as well as in those with whom I come in contact, is a fundamental dimension of a Christian principle-centered existence.

    These examples of how our core selves can and do determine who we are and the world in which we live are the results of choices made by us. Being a Christian is not a passive happening that flows from our baptism and our obedience to particular rules. Being a Christian is most fundamentally revealed in the moment-by-moment choices of the meanings we choose to shape who we are and how we see our world. Each moment of our lives we choose an orientation or set of meanings through which we engage reality. In each lived moment, we are called to see ourselves, our world, and those we share it with as God sees them, to behold ourselves and each other with the dignity and sanctity of a child of God, a temple of his spirit and life. This does not happen without consciousness and will.

For most human beings, this posture of reframing or maintaining a rightful spiritual core requires two major disciplines. The first, and in some ways the most difficult, is the decision to live in the moment, i.e., to truly be present to myself and my environment right now. So many of us live either six steps ahead or as many steps behind. We are either worried about the past, which has long ceased to be, or are projecting ourselves into a future, which has not come and may never be. The problem with both of these life stances is that God exists in the present moment, which is the only real moment of life. God's grace and strength are here, now for the believer and not in the past or in some possible future. Jesus made this clear when he advised his disciples and those following him, "Therefore do not be anxious about tomorrow, for tomorrow will be anxious for itself. Let the day's own trouble be sufficient for the day" (Matthew 6:34).

The second discipline that we must embrace, if we are to live a principle-centered existence and in particular a Christian-centered life, is to continuously engage with the source of these principles and values through reading and reflecting on Jesus's life and message. For how can we hold to a specific principle-centered life based on Christ without our continued encounter with his life, teachings, and example? Our continual formation is also discovered in both our private and public prayer and in our continuous humble assessment of ourselves in light of his message and call. The principle-centered life is also deeply enriched through the discovery of truths found in other religions, with spiritual traditions manifesting God's universal truth.

It is amazing to perceive the degree in which the spirituality that undergirds human religions is seamless. The essential truths embodied not in religions, but in the spirituality that is their foundation, reveal more commonality than difference. This commonality is the truth we all seek and that calls each of us forth within the traditions appropriate to our place and time. Together, the two disciplines of living in the moment and of continuously renewing our proper orientation based on God's word, which speaks to us through various sources such as life, holy books, and lives of great persons, are the continual sources of rediscovery of what is true and who we are. Our ongoing heartfelt assessments of our choices are essential precursors for us to more fully incarnate the meanings that bring life, hope, and light to a world that is ours to redeem. It is through this opening up of oneself to the principles, meanings, and values that one aspires to incarnate that we begin the process of training our wills in enabling us to be free.

The Capacities Inherent in Humanity and What They Make Possible

Beginning, as we have done, by saying that we are creatures among creatures is a significant first step in understanding ourselves. Both creation myths within Genesis are explicit in saying that we are not the sole creations of God. Everything that shares our world was made as we were and was declared good. Certainly, biblical tradition gives human beings a place of primacy in creation, but this should never be confused with a fundamental separation from the basic dust that formed us all and thus acts as the common link between humanity, the world, and all its many creatures.

The symbolism of the creation of Adam from the very same dust from which all of creation was formed is both powerful and essential.

This dust or chaos that God breathes life into is in fact the same chaotic dust that God calls life into via his evocation of "Let there be" (Genesis 1:3) contained in the creation story of the universe. In one image, God is using his breath (Genesis 2:4, 7–8) to convey his spirit of life (breathing life into Adam) and in another, his Word (*logos*, used both in the creation of the cosmos and in the incarnation). Both of these images will carry forward as key symbols of God's continued life-giving methods. In fact, after the resurrection of Jesus, he met the disciples in the closed upper room and according to John 20: 19–23, he breathed on them and gave them the supreme gift of the Holy Spirit.

To grasp what it is to be human, one must ground the notion of humanity within the very bedrock of creation and, more specifically, within the appreciation that humans can only be understood within the context of this world, their world. In short, we are dust called forth into being by the Word and the breath of God. The Word, which is the perfect, efficacious expression of God's generativity, generosity, love, and his breath, which is his very Spirit that not only imparts initial life but sustains that life in each of us, are the essential vivifying elements of all of creation.

The initial forming of this reflection posited the ordered laws of nature as a fundamental pre-requisite for a world in which freedom could exist. The laws of nature not only determined how the world would evolve, but were crucial to the necessary capacity of humans to be capable of exercising their wills freely. For the laws of nature and the capacity of human freedom expressible through their wills required the conjoining of the regular and anticipatable happenings of existence and the probable outcomes of human choices. Through this marriage of seeming opposites, freedom of the human will and the rigid laws of nature, the necessary requirement of accountability and responsibility were born. With this structure in place, God's gift of the will to humanity would become an effective tool provided to humans to participate in the salvation of themselves and their world.

Before we can move ahead with our reflection and the role of the unique aspects given to humanity for the ultimate achieving of God's plan, it is necessary that we describe the major capabilities of human existence. This will ensure better clarity as we progress. All humans are comprised of three major elements: their bodies, souls, and agency. The human body is that which situates us in time and place. It serves as the referencable aspect of a specific individual. I recognize Sally by recognizing her body or her voice. The body comprises a number of organs, including our brains, which act as the central control system for maintaining our physical beings. Our brains control the autonomous functions of breathing, control the levels of sugar or insulin in our blood, and various other unconscious activities required for our continued existence. Our brains also control our capacities to express ourselves verbally, in writing, and with gestures. Our brains additionally are the centers for the storing of our memories down to remarkable levels of detail including smells and sounds. The brain is also the central point of cognition or thinking. The brain provides humans with the ability to imagine, create symbols, analyze and understand those symbols, as well as most of what we usually associate with cognition.

Human beings also have life, which we will attribute to our souls. The soul, as it is being used here, is not a thing. It is not like a driver that sits in the truck and thus is responsible for the movement of the vehicle. The soul is the existence that animates the body. The soul not only is the principle of animation but also the principle of each person's unique self. What this means is that the soul is the source of one's personal consciousness. Consciousness is minimally understood as the source of our ability to say "I." It is the source of our capacity to be aware of things, myself, and others. Consciousness is always of something. It is thus directional. Consciousness thus always has an object to which it is focused, no matter whether this thing is external to the individual or an idea or feeling within the individual. Each individual's consciousness is unique to that particular individual and is a fundamental source of their concept of themselves.

Every human also has a soul as the source of his or her vitality. As well as being the principle of their life, the soul is the repository of the individual's self. Human vitality thus is not just the manifestation of life through brainwaves and our pulse, but it is the source and ground of our individuality that is expressed in our consciousness. Human consciousness is first and foremost the capacity to own my identity and to express this ownership in the use of self-referring pronouns and specifically my name. Human consciousness is more than this, however. The soul of a human also has an additional capacity, and that is the ability of the individual to be conscious of something particular and simultaneously to be conscious of one's self as being conscious of that particular thing. This is called our reflexive consciousness, for it is an aspect of consciousness that enables us to bend back and be aware of ourselves as being simultaneously aware of something else. For example, I may be at a dance and be conscious of seeing some of my friends and at the same time be very conscious of myself as uncomfortable or uneasy because I feel inadequate as a dancer. The first conscious stream is focused on the environment and finding friendly faces. The second is focused on my inward states as uneasy and awkward. This is one's reflexive consciousness. More of this will be described as we continue. This unique space created by the human capacity to be conscious of something and at the same time aware of its own state is essential in understanding the will and how it operates in human experience.

The third element of being human is human agency. Human agency is derived from the inter-relationship between the body and its principle of animation and consciousness, the soul. Human agency is the capacity of humans to will or choose. It is the seat of our freedom as well as the space in which this freedom operates. It is also the inherent driver of our need and ability to create meaning. In this way human agency is not an organ or any other physical thing, per se. It is a capacity born from the integration of our bodies and the principle of our existences and source of our concept of self.

These elements of being human will be critical to our continued reflection. It should now be clear that if we are discussing a person's capacity to do algebra, we are focusing on our cognitive or mental functions. If we are speaking about how a person experiences life and themselves, we are speaking about aspects of the body, the soul, and human agency as they work together to integrate external and internal experiences and then most importantly determine their meaning, and from these take appropriate actions.

It is now necessary that we continue our reflection on the specifics involved in what is entailed in life from the perspective of humans. This will entail a shift in perspective from perceiving the world as a stage we passively experience and upon which actions take place to an appreciation that the freedom we have discussed has a material role in the world each of us lives in, and the selves we also create through the exercising of this freedom. The world is more than the contextual framework in which humans, as free beings, exist. The world is the living context in which God's creation as an ongoing process continues. As such, the act of creation that is expressed in the Old Testament and in many other mythologies does not, in our view, represent a complete or finished action. Our lives and the creation of the world are not completed entities, but complex realities that are in process. The seventh day in Genesis did not represent the absolute finality of creation, but represented a major chapter in creation—just as our births did not represent our completed coming into being, but only an initial phase in our unfolding.

The relationship between each individual and the world within which each dwells is a fundamentally specific and intimate exchange. While it would be absurd to hold that there is no world out there in which we live and discover ourselves, it is also equally naïve to suggest that this world is some completely discoverable, objective reality knowable from outside the context of human experience. Truly understanding our humanity requires that we be conscious of the additional complexities that exists in our interactions with the world as the result of the active participation we have in our own and the world's continued unfolding. In short, it is critical that we grasp the creative dimensions of human experience and not just the receptive aspects of our experiences. Discovering the nature of the passive and active dimensions at the heart of our unique ways of being is essential in discovering the full dimensions of human life.

To make this explication as accessible as possible, it is essential to divide reality into two major categories. The first category is what we think of as what we perceive or experience. For simplicity, let's refer to this aspect of the world and ourselves as *the given*. By "given" we mean that which exists independent of our wills and which we accept as the way it is. The given is the aspect of reality that we accept as "out there" and that we often believe we are passive in experiencing.

The second aspect of any perception is the portion of our perceptions that is active. These dimensions of perception are real and inseparable from passive experiences. The active participation of human beings in experiences is not something most of us think about in our ordinary day-to-day living, but this does not negate its significance in describing our ways of being and experiencing this world. As many of us learned in our first year of philosophy in college, some experiences such as color, taste, smell, and sounds are how the human body interprets certain external stimuli. Specifically, this means that color, or saltiness, or the glories of Beethoven's Fifth Symphony are the results of how our optical nerves, taste buds, and auditory canals interpret specific kinds of stimuli. Thus, the answer to the age old conundrum of whether a tree falling in the woods with no one around to hear it would make any noise is no. It would make waves that would be able to produce noise on an appropriate auditory receptor only found in certain organisms.

This is in no way meant to question the veracity of our experiences. Rather, it is meant to acknowledge that all perception is an interaction between two realities, a subject (person) and an object (thing), or even between two subjects. It is this dialectic between the world as "given"—concrete, real—and the self as not merely a receptor but most essentially as also a creator, which contains the secret of the abundant possibilities and the corollary responsibilities for us as human beings. In order to understand what is being stated and that what might at first glance appear very abstract requires a careful reflection on life and what is really happening within the process of our living and our having experiences.

All animate things share life but not to the same degree or in the same manner. The ability of beings to move, adapt, respond to, and engage reality varies with the particular creature being examined. Humans have a very developed capacity to interact with the world. Our bodies are capable of many wonders of agility and strength. Our minds provide us with the capacity to reason, to be creative, and therefore to adapt to a wide variety of external realities. In this way the mind enables us to transcend the given aspects of our physicality by making us capable of modifying the external world in such a way as to be more amenable to our needs. Together, our minds and bodies create a strength that is far greater than either considered in isolation. To define humans as minds and bodies, however, would be an incomplete picture. As we have noted above, both our souls and the agency that is born of the highly integrated nature of body and soul are essential to a complete understanding and appreciation of the wonder of humanity and its role in salvation history.

The complete view of the human person entails aspects of reality that need to be uncovered. The dual aspects of human consciousness and the capacity to interpret experience, which enables humans to impose meanings on everything they experience, introduces a space within human experience that is unique and essential to our understanding of our place in this world. It is this space that enables humans to question and wonder. It is this space that is central to our capacities to experience our moods, fears, hopes, and joys. It is also what enables us to ruminate about life, our existence, and its meaning, as well as our blessings and our experiences of wonder and mystery. It is highly probable that this space is the foundation for our ability and indeed our need to be artistic and creative. Most importantly, it is within this space that humans transcend having mere experiences but now become active participants in the experiences we have.

Up until now, the word *space* has been used to convey a distance from our perceptions that makes possible our not just having an experience, but actually participating in the experience we are having via our emotions, hopes, and ways of looking at life, such as faith. It has uncovered a key to grasping the essential aspect of human existence. It is an imperfect descriptor as we move forward, conveying an emptiness that is anything but true. For this distance from our perceptions that enables us to actively participate in the perception itself is not empty. It can be filled with fear, prejudice, worry, indifference, generosity, concern, hope, and an infinite number of other realities. Whatever fills this space has a contributive aspect to what we perceive and how we react to or ignore significant aspects of our world. Humans, therefore, take consciousness a step further than any other creature, for we are conscious of ourselves as conscious of something else, and this consciousness that I am and bring to every situation is essential in understanding not only what I perceive, but more importantly, who I am and how I perceive what I experience.

Consciousness and its ability to bend back on the self are what characterize uniquely human awareness. Simple consciousness that is shared by many creatures is always directional and single threaded, i.e., it always has an object to which it is attached. For many of the world's creatures, consciousness is of the prey they are pursuing or the ball that they are seeking to fetch. This consciousness can also be of an internal awareness of an injury or illness. Human consciousness differs in that it is an awareness that colors one's perceptions.

For purposes of clarity, we have broken up our consciousness into multiple threads. This is not how it is actually experienced by us most of the time and thus may be helpful as a tool of explanation but not necessarily in line with how we experience it and ourselves. We do actually have the ability to have multiple simultaneous threads to our consciousness. For example, I am presently aware of my ideas about this paper and my exposing these ideas via this computer keyboard, while at the same time, I am aware and conscious of numerous household tasks which I have not addressed even though I promised to do so. What makes this unique quality of human consciousness so critical to our understanding of ourselves and our comprehension of our lives is that it brings the space at the core of human experience to the fore as the opportunity for the exercise of our essential capacities.

A key outcome of this unique capacity of human consciousness to bend back upon itself is the human capacity to give meaning to the events of our lives (e.g., to wonder, meditate, and to give meaning to oneself, situations, other people, and the world writ large). Our two-pronged consciousness is both blessing and curse, for it enables humans to acutely experience the richness of existence, and yet it also compels us to understand and make sense of this life. It is this self-reflexive aspect of our consciousness that makes so many of us unfulfilled with just a full belly, a warm bed, and no fear of immediate danger. It is this gift that compels us to wonder and seek the meaning of ourselves and our world. In many ways, it is this self-reflexive aspect of humans that underlies our capacity for freedom, as well as our drive for something more. This second prong of consciousness is also the essential key in understanding human existence with its unique capacities, responsibilities, and purpose.

Humans are thus not just conscious of the object being perceived but of themselves as the subject perceiving. It is this self-reflexive aspect of humanity's consciousness that is unique. This "I" that I am, which is present and aware in each act of perception, is not a mere *tabula rasa* or blank tablet upon which perceptions impose themselves, as Locke once postulated. This self-reflexive "I" does more than just record events or stimuli. It does more than merely stitch together images and sensations as the creative matter of our imaginations and dreams. The act of perception is more than just mere passive observation of either the self's internal states or ideas or the external world with which it interacts. This self-reflective stance of my consciousness is the source of the human capacity to be aware of this self as introspective and thus as having peculiar *internal dispositions* that can meaningfully alter how one experiences oneself, one's world, and everything that goes on between the two. These predispositions of the self can include being aware of oneself as insecure, sad, joyful, cynical, afraid, in awe, feeling inferior, and an infinite number of other internal dispositions independent of the particular events in which I may find myself. As such, the second prong of consciousness transforms human perception from passive to active.

As has been noted, this self-reflexive awareness is not empty but is the receptacle of my identity which is both what is, or "given," and what I create through acts of my will. It is another aspect of human existence that is fundamentally unique. It completely alters how humanity exists in the world, for it means that humans are active in the act of perceiving. Humans receive material input either as internal or external perceptions, but how these external perceptions become what each of us experiences is fundamentally unique to each individual. Other creatures that share this world differ from us in this fundamental respect. My dog, Harry, for example, is aware of his world. He is aware of me and of the rabbits he chases and the ball with which we play. He is not aware of himself as aware of these. He does not reflect on his state as he does these various things. Questions of mood, meaning, loss, the value of the rabbit, and the rabbit's loved ones do not course through Harry's mind as he leaps to grab the rabbit. Harry does not, like a golden retriever version of Camus, ponder the potential existential absurdity of this continued cycle of rabbit chasing, ball chasing, and waiting for his master's return from work. Harry does not experience his life through this layer of internal messages, which makes Harry's way of being in the world less multidimensional than his human companion's. Harry participates in the world, but unlike humans, Harry is not truly active in shaping the world in which he lives. What becomes critical to understand is just what is different and what this means and if there is purpose in this difference.

We have already noted that human consciousness as described above is not merely a passive capacity that enables the observation of the world; it is essential at this point to reflect upon and understand the full impact of this capacity upon our natures. Human consciousness is most importantly the action of the human will in creating the world it perceives. This creative capacity is the active choice of how each of us experiences events, ourselves, and other people. In more formalized language, it is the active capacity of the human will which expresses the central agency of the human person through ongoing constructive acts of creation. Jean-Paul Sartre wrote a famous play entitled *No Exit*. In this play, a group of people are thrown together into a nondescript room with two couches and a door, which in time they will discover leads to nowhere. During the course of the play, the observer is provided the opportunity to watch as each of the characters takes this very bland setting and these very different people now forced together and transforms it into a living hell.

For Sartre, two critical elements are essential for the observer. The first is that the hell that soon emerges is a direct result of the choices of the people within it and secondly that there is no escape. This second factor is an interesting element to ponder. It could be a symbol of our world, from which there is equally no escape, or it could point to the fact that the room is merely a context and is really not a player but a device used to magnify the centrality of the choices of each of the characters as the single essential factor of what ends up being created.

When we perceive anything—a situation, an object of art, a person, or a situation between people on the street, a beautiful sunset, whatever it may be—we participate in what we actually perceive. As I reflect on something that happened at work, I imbue this event with an entire set of personal meanings. These meanings truly make that event both a sharable happening (with those who may have been there as well) but also fundamentally my own experience. It is often through dialogues with others that we are provided an opportunity to modify our personal perception of an experience and, in some cases, come closer to a less distorted view. In other cases, we may bring the group perception closer to our experience. The consciousness that is central to who we are as humans is a kind of active lens through which each of us engages our worlds, ideas, thoughts, and emotions. This metaphor of a lens, while helpful, is limited because a lens is passive and static, and it engages only one of our senses. Wearing a pair of blue glasses would determine that anyone doing so would see the world with a blue tint. The human capacity to create that determines the world one lives in is dynamic, changeable, and a central expression of the agency of the individual. It also involves all of our senses and thus affects our experiences on multiple levels.

At this juncture, it is important that an additional aspect of what we have been reflecting upon—our active capacities in perceiving—be made more explicit. Not only does each person participate in the external experiences that they have, but even more importantly, each of us turns this creative lens upon our very selves and with it the constructive aspect of creating the self that I am. How I perceive myself, in the same manner that I perceive anything external, is a creative act that, while not always conscious, is an essential facet of perceiving. If a central meaning through which I discover myself, other people, and interpret situations is fundamentally cynical, then that filter is expressing a central aspect of how I am, who I am, and how I see myself. The external cynicism may be the expression of my internal self-loathing. Who I am at my core is not merely the wiring I inherited and the happenings that have filled my life at any point, but more importantly, the picture that these elements enable me to create of myself.

This work began by looking at how humanity is constructive of the perceptions it has. This choice of starting with external perceptions, while being existentially upside down, was chosen because it is easier to explain and comprehend than the primary reality that who

I am in my own inner eye is the real author of why I see the world one way and you another. As young children, we all absorb external messages about ourselves with a minimal filter. It takes many of us years to discard those messages that are not who we are or want to be, but deal with them we must. Adolescence is the most intense period of self-creativity as the young person battles everything in an attempt to create an individual identity. Some aspects of past learning's habits and views may be tossed aside only in later years to be reacquired but now as my own.

As has already been acknowledged, a significant portion of our identities are passed on to us as givens. What is being highlighted here and what is the most important aspect is that neither the givens nor anything else can determine who I am but my will to determine how I will integrate and make sense of myself. It is in this context that the claim that God created in seven days and that each of our lives began with the tears of our mother's labor is significantly limited. For both God and our mothers set in motion a process of creation that continues even today and for each of us will be ongoing until our deaths. My life, my very identity, has only one true author and that is me. It is the sole reason why God wanted humanity to have a will. It is the very basis for truly understanding the message of Jesus and the many other prophets that have called out to us time and time again to bring the kingdom of God to this, our world, as a true capability and vocation.

It is in this way that our spiritual dimensions of humanity are both dependent on our acceptance of our human capacities and an understanding of their critical role in developing the people we become and are. It is also essential that these capacities be recognized as materially impactful on our perceptions and the actions that flow from them. The truth of this flow from experience to meaning to perception and then to action is all too real, and its ramifications make themselves evident not only in each of our lives, if we look hard enough, but also in our history.

The pattern is a common one: a member of a minority is in a situation where an individual or group of individuals perceives their presence as threatening, unusual, or unacceptable. As a result, a series of actions unfolds that result in escalating tensions and, at times, violence. In the end, what is discovered is that the underlying problem was the presumed meanings of the participants about the minorities and their intentions. The reason is that the individual frame of reference or consciousness, as we have been calling it, has been formed from very different experiences. Excluding pure hate crimes, often crimes of fear are the result of assumptions based on the meanings of the participants involved.

At a purely human level, one can see that our consciousness is primary when trying to understand ourselves and how we experience the lives we live. Happiness, fulfillment, boredom, meaninglessness, cynicism, despair are all examples of outcomes that derive from the world and the self we create. Our expectations of life, ourselves, others, God, our government are all wound up in the self and world we knit together. Many might argue that this is true but trivially so. Who isn't aware of their role in their perceptions of life? If this were the case, wouldn't we spend more time educating ourselves and our children on being more conscious of this central dimension of human existence? Wouldn't the need for our conscious awareness and acceptance of this capacity within our own lives be something we would expend far more energy upon if we truly grasped this?

Our Christian lives build on our humanity. Christianity neither covers up nor expunges our basic human existence. The message of Jesus was about the correct application of the capacities given to humanity in creation. The capacity for each of us to bring the kingdom into reality here on this earth was central to Jesus's message. "The kingdom of God is not coming with signs to be observed; nor will they say, 'Lo, here it is!' or 'There!' For behold, the kingdom of God is in the midst of you" (Luke 17: 20–21). Certainly, this text references Jesus himself as the very special manifestation of humanity in its perfect openness to God's plan, but could it also be making the point that the kingdom is as close as our willingness to make it present through our co-creative active participation in the world and our own continual process of becoming?

Later, Jesus compares the kingdom of God to a mustard seed, this smallest of seeds which becomes one of the largest of bushes and is able to support a multitude of life (Matthew 13:31–32). Is this small but mighty seed a metaphor for the seemingly insignificant choices that each person makes every day of their lives, which if they flowed from a more complete sense of who one is and what one's relationship with the world is, could transform the world itself? If so, then what is this more complete view of the person? Are there clues to the aspects of our self-creation, which by informing our beings can bring us and the world closer to the kingdom Jesus references? For a Christian, one of the most famous articulations of Jesus' message of a right-oriented perspective is encapsulated in the Sermon on the Mount. What is being articulated here is a set of principles that, if formative of our chosen ways of being, can do nothing short of reorienting our fundamental meanings and values.

> Blessed are the poor in spirit, for theirs is the kingdom of heaven. Blessed are they that mourn, for they shall be comforted. Blessed are the meek, for they shall inherit the earth. Blessed are those who hunger and thirst for righteousness, for they shall be satisfied. Blessed are the merciful, for they shall obtain mercy. Blessed are the pure in heart, for they shall see God. Blessed are the peacemakers, for they shall be called the sons of God. Blessed are those who are persecuted for righteousness' sake, for theirs is the kingdom of heaven. Blessed are you, when men revile you and persecute you and utter all kinds of evil against you falsely on my account. Rejoice, and be glad, for your reward is great in heaven; for so men persecuted the prophets who were before you.
>
> Matthew 5:3–12 (RSV)

After espousing this beautiful but disturbing inversion of how most of us consider being blessed, Jesus then proclaims to those gathered around him that they, imperfect human beings, are the salt of the earth (Matthew 5:13–14) as well as the light of the world (Matthew 5:14–17). Jesus is once again juxtaposing the people we can be in opposition to the people we are. He is forcing us to look inward and discern how our lived choices are bringing us closer to the image God created us to be, or not. He also warns us about letting the salt lose its taste or keeping our light concealed from those surrounded in darkness, for both eradicate the possibility of a life fully lived and the possibility of being partners in the salvation of this world and each other. We are the salt that gives richness and flavor to each other's lives and the light that clears away the darkness and the shadows of loneliness, sadness, alienation, and hopelessness.

Jesus is warning us that we cannot escape ourselves and our cocreative wills. He is declaring our mission, but he is also forcing each of us to accept our personal freedom provided in our ability to will. He is acknowledging our capacity to listen but not hear, to look but not see, and worst of all, to forget who we are as sons and daughters of the Father. For what is a world without light? What is life without salt, but stale and unsatisfying, dark, lonely, and empty of beauty? Again in the same section of Matthew, Jesus makes absolutely clear what he is really addressing when he says:

> You have heard that it was said to the men of old, 'You shall not kill; and whoever kills shall be liable to judgment.' But I say to you that everyone who is angry with his brother shall be liable to judgment; whoever insults his brother shall be liable to the council, and whoever says 'You fool!' shall be liable to the hell of fire.
> Matthew 5:21–23, 27–30 (RSV)

This entire sermon once again shifts the expected perspective. In this case, it is a shift from actions to our inner dispositions. The anger and lust that Jesus is using as examples point to how we as individuals internally devise our ways of being in relationship. The underpinning of this radical ethic is that we must alter our way of being in the world, which is driven by our formative self-concepts, and only subsequently by the actions that flow from them. Certainly, murder and fornication are far more serious than the anger and lustful thoughts one can often be party to. If we fail to understand the linkage between these internal dispositions which we choose and which form the kind of persons we become, then the actions that often flow from them are merely the logical outcomes of the many points of freedom which preceded.

This passage is meant to shock us back into consciousness. How and what we perceive and the perspectives that imbue them, whether of hate, prejudice, invincibility, or victimhood are our acts of will and play themselves out in our words, actions, and ways of living. This passage and the one cited before it are calls to humanity to wake up and to own our lives, to own who we are and where we are going. Jesus is demanding that each of us harness the gift of freedom that undergirds our very beings and recreate ourselves based on a new set of principles and values. This view of the specific vocation of each Christian can also be understood as the basis for the enigmatic saying of Jesus that in order to enter heaven, one must be born again. This rebirth in the Spirit needs to be understood as the reclaiming of our images based in the mind of God before we were conceived through the responsible acceptance of the underlying choices that define our very beings.

Up to this juncture we have focused, and rightly so, on the creative aspects of our human lives as co-creators of our very selves and the world we occupy. It is essential, though, that we not take this too far. Human beings are social beings first and foremost. It is this fundamental aspect of our natures as social beings that ensures the creative aspects of our perceptions do not drive us toward utter individuality and solipsism, but ensures that our experiences and perceptions always remain within a range of normalcy determined by the social constructs in which we exist. As a community, we are self-correcting. It is this that saves us from a radical solipsism or subjectivism. Society is the regulator of the normative boundaries of perceptual deviations.

This collective model of perception is not new and is only being addressed here to provide the proper context for establishing a description of how human agency or will is involved in our fundamental perceptions of ourselves and of the world in which we live. The idea that we as humans can actually get at happenings as they are in themselves is what has been called in academic circles *naïve realism*. It is the lack of appreciation that one can never perceive anything without ourselves as the perceivers. That means that I bring the totality of my experiences, beliefs, fears, hopes, disappointments, and expectations to each episode in my life. I also bring the structures of my physical nature that enable me to have certain kinds of sensory experience. More holistically, each person brings not just their individual experiences, but also the cultural-contextual experiences of their community to every perception as part of what informs each of these from happenings to experiences. The world, and by that is now meant specifically other people, places, creatures, things, and the situations they populate, is not an independent happening to which one merely responds. Humans are the co-authors of the world in which they live, work, and the creators of their cultures and history.

Every day, we experience the reality that we in fact live in radically different worlds than some of the people with whom we have daily contact. What may be unclear is how substantive this notion of different worlds is and what its consequences can be for us individually, as societies, and as a species. It is not difficult to substantiate the claims being put forth here that these internal choices of how we see and perceive can and have had dire consequences for humanity. It was not so long ago that slavery and segregation were considered normal. Nineteenth-century scientists filled volumes arguing the sub-humanity of various cultures. It has not even been one hundred years since the anti-Semitism of Europe and America enabled one of the most horrific episodes in history, the Holocaust. These actions began as ways of seeing and perceiving and ultimately expressed themselves in actions for which all humanity is guilty. In these modern times, we still have this same reality percolating around the globe, whether based on culture, creed, sexual orientation, or gender. It is critical for us to expose how it is that we create our selves and the communities we each inhabit as highly personal realities. It is clear that the individual self that we are and the world that we each inhabit are not merely external realities that we experience as they are. They are in significant ways the direct result of our wills, our choices, and thus infuse our perceptions and the actions that flow from them whether as individuals or as nation-states.

Even as we focus on this transcendent nature of our beings, the biblical myth of dust as the grounding element of our being is the best image to make apparent our integrated connectedness as an integrated element of creation in its entirety. This fact should temper our lofty appreciation of our place within the miracle of salvation and redemption by rooting us in the very basic *Urstuff,* or grounding in, our world as dust. Thus, how we treat this home, which is ourselves, should be vitally important to us. Unfortunately, many of us persist in perceiving our relationship to the world as that of a pin stuck into a globe. Certainly, the pin is related to the globe and should be concerned about the globe, but implied within this image is the sense that one could somehow get unstuck and move on if one had to. A very clear picture of humanity's relationship to this world, which is radically different than that of the pin in the globe, is being postulated. In fact, it would not be an overstatement to say that humanity is *of* the world, not *on* it. The world is the single context in which humanity is possible. The relationship, therefore, is not incidental but necessary. The image of the pin is thus not just unfortunate, it is potentially dire, for it could have disastrous consequences for us if not exposed and questioned before it is too late. This fundamental position is also at the heart of a Christian's belief that Christ's coming and the giving of God's Spirit is a call to redeem not just ourselves as individuals or as humanity, but also the rest of creation. It is at the core of the belief that the resurrection is not merely a spiritual reawakening but the raising of our total beings both material and spiritual.

There are other critical dimensions of humanity that must also be exposed in order to continue this journey of discovery of our uniqueness, our potential, and our vocation. The next dimension of being human that is an essential aspect of ourselves was developed in the thought of Martin Heidegger, a German philosopher of the twentieth century. Heidegger focused on the fact that humanity as "self-reflexive consciousness" exists in time. This idea, as with many of Heidegger's ideas, can be very abstract. As a method of providing clarity, therefore, literature has provided us a very real and poignant illustration of the relationship between our identity and our temporality. This wonderful description of the abstractions that would only much later be expressed by this German philosopher is captured in the small novella *A Christmas Carol*.

The story by Charles Dickens centers on a mean, stingy, odious old man whose name would come to characterize his very description: Scrooge. In this tale, Dickens weaves a story in which Scrooge's loathing for Christmas finally evokes the wrath or pity of the ghost of his partner, Jacob Marley. Jacob tells Scrooge that he has come on behalf of his reclamation and that his only hope is to be visited by three specters, the ghosts of his Christmases past, present, and future. Reluctantly, Scrooge relents. Through his journey into his own past, present, and future, Scrooge reacquires himself. His soul, and thus his hardened heart, is softened, and the spirit of the season is able to permeate and let in the light of truth with its warmth of hope and replaces the stone cold of fear and loneliness that have pervaded Scrooge's very identity. Dickens grasped that to understand a man one must understand not just who he is today, but who he was and who he longed to become. Having Scrooge face himself in his temporality forced him to open his eyes and face the multitude of choices he had made and the many ramifications of these choices for him and others from his past, in his present, and in his future.

Scrooge typifies many dimensions of what we are trying to expose about core aspects of our shared humanity. Scrooge, through many acts of his will over time, had chosen to close himself off from his world. In a real sense, Scrooge chose to create a smaller and smaller world in which his narrow existence was characterized by both internal and external stinginess, a lack of generosity of both spirit and resources. He neither noticed the real effects of his willed posture of self-centeredness nor its effects on the lives of those poor souls forced to interact with him. The ghosts forced Scrooge to face the ramifications of his choices—not just of his specific actions but also the ramifications of these choices for who he was becoming at each step and the effects on the people around him. These spirits made manifest to Scrooge the power of his will. Scrooge was forced to see and accept that his actions had profound consequences for him and the world he left behind. Waking from this experience, Scrooge realized that these same truths applied to the present and thus to his future. By recognizing the centrality of his will, he now could change for the better, just as he had created the world and self he had been forced to witness by the spirits of Christmas. Yes, Scrooge had a difficult father and lost a sister he dearly loved, but he now learned that the secret to life is in the meaning that one gives to these events and the choices one makes as a result.

A Christmas Carol provides an experiential method of getting at the core of Heidegger's thought. This aspect of ourselves that Heidegger raises to the level of our consideration is our need to understand time as an integral element of our self-reflexive consciousness, both as individuals and as societies. This insight attaches itself to the constructive elements of consciousness, which we have shown enables us to add to our perceptions and calls out the fact that the underlying meanings we impose on our personal experiences are created and recreated in the context of our lived time. Heidegger also propounds that time is also substantially interconnected with the past, present, and future of our culture, religion, family history, and society into which each of us has been born. In fact, Heidegger's great contribution to our understanding of ourselves was to enrich our appreciation of ourselves as "beings in time." It is essential to note that our perceptions of the world are indeed molded by centuries of influences. This fact will become critical for our development of the Christian person, for it brings forth the reality that the symbols (words, images, rituals) that are used as the building blocks for a unique Christian self-consciousness draw upon a rich cultural cache, composed initially by the inherited materials provided by a specific society, culture, and historical context.

Thus my self-reflexive consciousness is developed out of a unique historical foundation of symbolic building blocks inherently nuanced by time and place. This culture, which will be passed on to the emerging "selves" by the familial society, will express the present by appropriating the past through the meaning that it helps society to formulate about itself and its relationship to the world. This culture will also project a future that is manageable for the emerging self and filled with possibilities and hope, until this unfolding self can establish a core set of its own personally chosen meanings and values. This cultural worldview and our societal preconscious frame of references are critical parts of our understanding of human development. A key aspect of the individual is thus temporality. Temporality is central to how individuals experience themselves as unfolding consciousnesses and as expanding agents capable of choice and the free exercise of will. Temporality is also the individual's external formative societal context in which his/her reflexive understanding of whom he/she is and what kind of world he/she lives in is experienced.

Humanity cannot be discovered except by discovering the world in which it exists. Indeed, we began this journey with the theological premise that creation, as we know it, was put in place so that all of creation and humanity could adore the Creator. Humanity, in particular, has been given a unique capacity to love as an action of our will. Humanity was created with a will that could be exercised within this world in such a way that the results of any action would require the actor to be responsible and accountable for the act. Whether one adopts the German idealism that saw certain realities such as space and time and cause and effect as constructs of human intellection, or whether one accepts that cause and effect are fundamental aspects of a reality imbued with natural laws flowing from its author, the rational order of nature is the basis upon which humanity's will and associated actions can have meaning. Without humanity's acts of will having meaning, there is no chance that we could ever will to love. It is also the fundamental presupposition for our ability to both live the Christian call and participate in Christ's redemptive mandate.

The role of humanity's "will" is a central element in the creation of the self and of the world that the self discovers. These two aspects of humanity's power, and thus responsibility, are critical for us to understand in our attempt to gain a greater appreciation for who we are and what our responsibilities are to ourselves, each other, and future generations. This new dimension of human agency that we designate "will" enables us to be self-constructive and world-constructive and is the lynchpin for the concept of the person and his/her potential and associated responsibility. It is also the nexus in which humanity and creator can converge or diverge as the will acts either in line with God's plan or in opposition. In short, it becomes the opportunity for the individual's and our world's salvation or damnation, actualization or destruction. It provides the key to being able to grasp the answer to the question of what it means to live the good life and whether there is any kind of moral foundation that one can derive from a view of humanity based on a will to love. For those who are members of faith communities and believe in God, the construct of the human person being developed here will enrich and challenge our modern, sometimes bloodless, belief postures. By articulating the full richness and texture of our human nature as well as demonstrating the real intimacy between our human experience and what it means to experience the divine, the foreignness of God will be fundamentally questioned. In fact, it will become clear that this experience of alienation between humanity and God springs from the underlying alienation that exists among human beings and within our very selves.

Humanity—Space & Time, Abundance & Scarcity

In the eighteenth century, the German philosopher Immanuel Kant opened up our appreciation of humanity's participatory relationship to the world. Kant claimed that two fundamental aspects of any human experience, space and time, were not realities "out there," but aspects of ourselves that we add to any experience. Without going too far afield from our focus, let us simply recognize that Kant demonstrated that space is a necessary component of any human experience because it is the manner in which we organize our perceptions. It was the same for time. This discovery was critical in the further maturing of humanity's understanding of our inextricable participation in what for centuries was thought to be external and objective. Understanding both space and time as human constructs of experience that we create and impose on our perceptions means that they are important factors in distinguishing their secular meanings from Christian or spiritually informed meanings.

The secular modernistic notion of space is infinite, vast, and complex. It is a construct of ongoing and limitless extension in which each person becomes inconceivably small and insignificant. While it inspires awe in its endlessness, it also is terrifying in its sterility. Few of us experience space in this theoretical manner. Most human's sense of space is filled with trees, people, houses, and one could go on and on. When speaking of space, we need to be cognizant of its various perspectives. Our view of space is focused on our internal experience of space. As noted above, a major aspect of secular space is not only its vastness but also its scarcity. Even the notion of the space prevalent when focusing on the earth has slowly emerged as one of limited resources. The secular concept of our personal space is also often strongly characterized by scarcity. In its largest sense, one could understand the concepts of economics as the study of how we make choices in a world where not only are our own resources limited but so are the resources of our world.

This secular orientation toward space is pervasive and paints a picture of life as a grasping race for its limited resources. These resources are not just foodstuffs, but even more critically love, attention, concern, opportunities, as well as material things. The belief that there is only so much goodness, blessedness, and bounty and that one person's abundance will in some way mean another person's loss are at the heart of the secular view of the scarcity model of existence. We can often see this acted out when someone is promoted or given a unique opportunity. How many of us have heard the griping and mean-spirited whispers that are generated from the belief that the good fortune that has been given to one will in some way have been taken away from someone else? This scarcity model is also revealed in our desire to hoard, to have more than is needed, and thus in a very real sense, the fear of scarcity leads to scarcity.

The scarcity-based view of life also significantly influences our perceptions of God. Are the blessings we get of limited number and thus the opportunities for God's grace measured and liable to run out? If I mess up a relationship or opportunity, do I believe that what has been lost can never be recovered? Do we carry around in us a view of God that is based on a creator whose love and desire for our happiness has its limits?

This secular belief in scarcity is a framework erected on egoism as opposed to generosity. It is a pre-reflective fear that there cannot be enough abundance. Unfortunately, we have created a world that reinforces this fear. Scarcity as a life orientation is at the center of human weaknesses such as envy, jealousy, covetousness, stinginess, manipulation, and fear. Modern wealth rests on so very few individuals, and in some cases to such a degree, as to be absurd. Simultaneously, desperate want and ignorance abound. Our hoarding, our attempt to fill our grain houses or bank accounts with abundance may seem natural, but have we stood back and asked about the true nature of abundance? Is it in material things and wealth? Is it in those who truly love me and who I dare to love? Is how I define my abundance really meaningful? If my life were to end tomorrow, would my abundance be read out in a will or in the lives I have touched and allowed to touch me? We spend immense energy and dollars discussing and worrying about our material investments. How much joy do they bring to each of us, no less to others? Does the ratio of concern to payback make any rational sense? How much must I have to have enough?

In opposition to this secular notion of space, of a scarcity model to life, the Christian concept of space is one of abundance, one of limitless intimacy and care. In the Christian worldview, we are not specks of nothingness in an unending universe. We are, each of us, loved and cared for. Each person is known, sustained, and an intimate partner with God. God does not have a predetermined number of good things to offer us; rather, God has an infinite capacity for love, not just in abstraction, but for each of us as individuals. As Jesus desperately wanted to convey to his disciples and to us that "...even the hairs of your head are all numbered" (Matthew 10:30). God should not be thought of as some deity that throws us a preset number of blessings, which, if overlooked, is lost forever. Our Christian image should be one of God lofting infinite blessings over and over and only waiting for us to catch them. God intends that his creatures be fulfilled.

This sense of intentionality, which is the basis of our belief that we are here for a reason and that each person is vitally important, is in direct opposition to the secular, materialistic view of space and our place in it. While it would be incorrect to state that Christianity supports or delineates a specific economic model as right or wrong, it would also be counter to the early Christian communities to say that there is not an economic ramification to Christ's message. As is described in the Acts of the Apostles, the early Church formed a social and economic model based on communalism (not communism). This model was the direct practical result of Jesus's teachings about mutual care, responsibility, and community. Communalism is vastly different than communism or socialism in that it is first and foremost a way of being and of perceiving my place in the world based on a belief in the worth of each individual and a core sense of responsibility to love our neighbor. It is the specific implementation of the Great Commandment and the church's identity as the people of God. It is less about a political model and more about the values that were pervasively at the center of Jesus's teaching.

Our concept of our spiritual internal space is equally opposed to the secular view. Our capacity to discover the abundance that comes from our ability to exercise our co-creative power by transcending the mundane realities that fill our lives by choosing the meanings we give to these realities is the essence of our internal space. Humans do not merely process events and perceptions. The meanings that permeate our inner space, such as the teachings of Jesus, focus on the opening of our senses so that we truly became attentive to each other. Thus our internal space is the place in which we discover the value of ourselves as well as each other. Once we become aware of the value of the other and the abundance of God's world, we are called to respond to what we experience with generosity and self-sacrifice. We are more than the mechanistic aspects of our beings. Discovering the freedom to be able to understand ourselves in this way and the courage to operate from this center of strength and nobility is not always easy. First and foremost, Christians must come to accept and experience the abundance that is God's love for them. It is from this realization that each of us is loved from the very depths of our being by God and that his supreme generosity neither diminishes nor trivializes his specific love of me as a unique individual or any other individual, which is the foundation of our ability to love as we are loved. God's love is also unconditional. There is nothing you could do that would separate you from God's love except your choice to reject it.

This realization of the abundance and magnificence of life can sometimes be hampered by the human experiences that surround our most vulnerable moments. Children are born into abusive families and never experience the safety that should be at the heart of the family or into situations where poverty imbeds a deep experience of not having enough, either as a result of war or the reality of poverty as something into which one is born. As a result, there may need to be a process of healing and grace that must precede the awakening of those scarred by poverty to become attuned to the abundance of the universe. It is a wonder of the human person that in many cases it is those who have come from so little that are truly aware of the riches of their lives that are not material, but just as precious in their families and in those with whom they share their lives. Once again, it is not the happenings or givens so much as the meanings which determine how the seemingly poorest can manifest a wealth deeper and richer than those blessed with material abundance.

Through this experience of being so loved we also come to discover our capacity to love. This concept of abundance is at the heart of the call of the Christian to give himself or herself away, to be generous. How many of us secretly live in a world in which we believe in life's scarcity and not its abundance? The inherent understanding that Christian space is at the same time intimate and abundant is essential to developing a right orientation to our world and a real appreciation for ourselves. Understanding this difference between secular space and Christian space is critical to our ability to be people of hope. It is true that our everyday experiences in this life often seem to contradict the notion of abundance. One person wins the lottery and everyone else doesn't; one person gets promoted and others do not. Often because of how we see these things, we miss our blessings and our experience of life's abundance because our focus is on another's good fortune as an implied personal loss. Few of us reflect on those periods of our life which have been particularly painful and in which we may have felt lost only later to grasp the pivotal role it played in preparing us for what was yet to come. There is a humility and a trust required of us to be positioned to learn the lessons that what might have seemed a disaster at one moment may ultimately be the key to unlocking multiple dimensions of life and love.

Time is another critical aspect of how we construct the meaning of our world and ourselves. The secular notion of time is linear. It begins with creation and moves infinitely outward to some ultimate end. A secular view of human time begins with birth and ends with death. This secular concept of time has engendered a belief in the absurdity of human existence popularized by the twentieth century existentialists such as Camus, Sartre, and others. A Christian notion of time is certainly directional but also contains the cyclical dimensions of human experience and is thus best conceived of as an ascending spiral. This experience of time acknowledges the cyclical nature of life that each of us experiences in the patterns of the day: the cycles of the moon, the continual death of winter and the promise of life in spring, and finally the experience of the helplessness of birth, our growth in strength and agency in life, and then our return to the limitations with which we began in our old age.

As Christians, these cycles are not mere repetitions. Each day, while like the last, is inherently new. Through our openness to God's Spirit, we can discover in each new moment or day profound truths about ourselves and our world. Through the proper alignment of our wills to truth, beauty, and goodness, we can discover new meanings that alter our old ways of being and perceiving reality. The new that infuses the ascending spiral transforms the merely repetitive into an opportunity of continual discovery. The awareness, this being attuned to new ways of experiencing is the outcome of one's choice to live the will to love. This concept of time as an upward spiral fosters an orientation toward existence that gasps at the apparent renewal of nature, of life, as the doorway to a new and profound understanding of ourselves and our world in the rediscovery of life renewing itself in each of us.

Absurdity in the Christian view of time is the choice of blindness and stagnation, i.e., the choice of the individual to turn inward, to not engage with life, to reject the continued call to be present to and thus to be seen. This orientation of personal withdrawal, whether based on fear, stinginess of spirit, or cynicism, is the underlying cause of the experience of alienation and loneliness. It is a living suffocation. It is the choice of death over life. Each moment in a Christian's life is the opportunity for greater awareness of our capacities, born of a generosity of spirit. Physical death is not the only kind of death that humans experience. The withdrawal from life and its subsequent isolation and alienation results in the willed murders of our individual souls. "Do not fear those who kill the body but cannot kill the soul" (Matthew 10:28). Love—understood as the right orientation of our wills to choose the good that is presented to us in each moment as calls of personal self-sacrifice, generosity, courage, and service—is the only remedy for the soul's being crushed by isolation and alienation. Resurrection is not just a faith stance; it is also the real, lived outcome of a conversion of the will to engage life in service and love and the new life that emerges from this stance. Our capacity to continually be revitalized by life and our proper engagement with it stands as a foreshadowing of the hoped for rebirth promised in the resurrection.

The centrality of the human ability to give meaning to events and happenings as well as the givens of our lives is what converts these into real experiences. It is through our communal aspects of being that our experiences do not result in my isolated experiences. For one of the central roles of the community is as the ongoing determiner of what experiences appear outside the norm. Without this critical function of the community, we could each find ourselves isolated in our own little worlds. Human life, as understood within a Christian context, is a delicate balance between individual and community. In fact, the orthodox Christian position has always maintained that human beings are first and foremost communal in nature. The healthy individual is the product of a healthy communal context, usually defined as the nuclear family. Without the proper communal construct, the individual human being has a highly unlikely chance of maturing into a healthy and fully enabled individual. This statement is grounded more deeply than in the mere practical aspects of the dependency of the infant on adults for food, clothing, and shelter. It is the acknowledgement of ourselves as grounded in the creation and understanding of ourselves as creatures who pass on, create, and make use of symbols for the continued communication and sharing of ourselves, our cultures, and our histories.

The act of giving meaning to ourselves, happenings, events and the many givens of our lives is the essential act of human beings creating themselves and the world in which they live. It is this active aspect of human existence that is the ground of our ability to participate in the continued redemption of ourselves and our world. Whatever meanings one may choose in the course of their lives, these meanings are determinative of who that person will be and how they will perceive their world and their role in it. These meanings are expressed through our symbols as well as our unique individual and communal stories. Each person is born into not just a family with its symbols and stories, but also into the larger cultural context of shared meanings expressed through social, ethnic, religious, and communal symbols. Our nature, as has been carefully articulated, is first and foremost communal. The family, being the smallest unit of communication of these building blocks of self-creation and personal identity, is the construct in which humanity's symbolic nature is fostered, nurtured, and produced Thus the symbols that are the basis from which we come to compose and then express meanings are part of the social milieu into which each of us is born. This does not mean to say that the meanings we end up accepting as mature individuals are determined, for certainly this is not the case. The symbolic constructs that each person uses in constructing their initial meanings are provided as part of the cultural context in which they were introduced. As we grow, experience life, obtain various levels of formal and informal education, our symbolic frame of reference expands and is personalized. Each individual ultimately creates his or her own context through which his or her unique worldview and self-understanding will emerge.

What is essential to grasp is that it is the *will* that is at the center of this creative process of choosing which symbols and which meanings will be the foundation of the individual's unique story. For some, there will be high a degree of self-awareness of this process right from the start. For others, this awareness may ebb and flow throughout their lives as they respond to the many moments of grace that call each of us to self-awareness. What is essential to understand is that each of us is responsible and accountable for the self and world that we create. While the degree of one's culpability can be significantly diminished due to many factors, it is critical to raise the fact that most of us have the capacities and the fundamental capabilities to accept the consequences of our actions and thus the responsibilities that accompany them. Like Scrooge from Dickens's tale, we must stay attuned to life's continued calling forth of our beings to know ourselves and to become more attuned to the life that calls us forth day in and day out. We must listen well to the many calls that are made each day in the course of our ordinary lives, in music, literature, and sacred rituals, as well as in our interactions with each other, that whisper to us to own our lives and then to give them away.

It is one of the wonders of our natures that as human beings we have an uncanny capacity for self-discovery in the negative. When a presupposition about life, the world, people, and ourselves gets challenged in the course of living, the veil of mystery that keeps us from seeing the truth about ourselves is often pulled away and our prejudices, blind spots, or presuppositions are exposed, and we are provided with an opportunity to face something about who we are or the world we have created that we would rather not see. Many of our central operating presuppositions are forced to the fore in these moments. These often-unsettling situations force us to experience that a large number of our perceptions have been painted with our own brush, our own hands, and our own paint. These moments can be epiphanies—moments of light or clarity, indeed moments of grace. It is at these times that a person is provided with the opportunity and the space to realign his or her ways of being. Initially, this may only take the form of a crack in the certainty about one's assumptions concerning one's self. It is often the case that these experiences can make apparent the difference in how we may perceive ourselves as opposed to how others perceive us. This realization can expose the many methods we have created to attempt to control our getting hurt by the creation of personae that acted as mechanisms to protect our vulnerability. These moments of grace may be the process of reawakening of vital sensitivities long ago abandoned. This initial fissure can be the first step in the process of eroding the entire edifice of false yet protective aspects of ourselves that one never knew were isolating and suffocating and not merely protecting the person desiring to live life to the fullest. In the broadest use of the term, these potential conversion experiences are not a narrow adopting of a certain formal creed, but a discovery of the truth of who one is, the acceptance of the world as it is, and the essential relationship between the two. Discovering the operating meanings, which are the shapers of who we are and what we experience and the actions and choices that emanate from these are prerequisites for obtaining personal authenticity.

One of the most poignant articulations of this human capacity to create meaning as an act of the will can be found in Viktor Frankl's *Man's Search for Meaning*. In this profound little book, Frankl presents the implications of humanity's capacity to choose the meanings that one gives to the events of life. His experience was one of humanity's most horrific—the concentration camps of the Holocaust. He observed people thrown into the same situation, and yet the outcomes of the lives of each person varied greatly, regardless of any external event. Excluding those occurrences where people were harmed by the actions of the Germans or other prisoners, some people withered and some people seemed to reach new levels of generosity of spirit and courage. Some people became more self-preoccupied, and it seemed as if their worlds became smaller while others in the same situation discovered the capacity to enlarge their worlds, to increase their awareness, and to tap into a level of personal generosity many never even knew they had. For many, this new openness was a way of being that they had never experienced before.

Frankl attributed this difference in each person's response to the same reality to only one thing: the diversity of how each individual finally chose to make sense of, or to give meaning to, the situations in which they were each placed. The choices they made and the meanings they chose not only changed how they viewed their situation, but how they viewed their fellow internees, their captors, and most importantly, themselves. This unfortunate, but very real practicum of the theories being espoused gives empirical credence to the role of the human will and meaning in the lives we live. The discovery of meaning as a fundamental, individual choice is at the very heart of our nature, our vocation, and our potential salvation, but it is critical to repeat that this capacity, while present, is not automatically evoked or realized. Grasping first that we have this capacity and its significance in our lives is one thing. Taking the steps to develop and strengthen our abilities to own our identities and thus our lives is the real journey one must decide to begin.

It should now be clear why this internal freedom to choose the meanings we give to our lives and the events within it are primary and our external choices—our liberties—are seen as secondary. For depending on how I see my world and myself, the actions and choices I make will be very different. My actions and external choices are thus truly derivative of the meanings they presuppose. The question that one may be asking is, "But are we truly free to determine the meanings we give to our world as well as ourselves? Aren't these also determined by how one is raised or the events of one's youth or one's health?" The answer is a resounding "no." Certainly severe mental incapacity could be a factor; however, this extreme anomaly should not be the basis for determining the perspective taken for the majority of human beings that have walked this earth, are living now, and are yet to be born. Even the most handicapped individual is always participative in the aspects of humanity that we have been discussing. They certainly may be limited in their expression or communication, but this does not mean that the capacity is not present.

The basis for the unequivocal acceptance of our responsibility and accountability for who we choose to be is born out in the countless lives lived and the stories that have survived of people who have willed themselves to transcend unbelievable constraints, limitations, experiences, and cruelties to somehow flower into something truly awe inspiring. All anyone has to do is to read any of the hundreds of thousands of biographies and autobiographies that have been written about ordinary men and women who have lived extraordinary lives, not because of the perfect conditions of their environments from birth or their extraordinary talents, but rather resulting from their unique "spirits" as expressed in their determinations, choices, and sacrifices, i.e., their wills and their freedom to determine the meanings they gave to their unique constraints. No, there is no condition one can describe that has not been met head-on and transcended via humanity's ability to choose meanings that not only enable survival but actually foster life, growth, and love at the most extraordinary levels of human capacity.

The ability to will the meanings that undergird the very self that I am, as well as the world that I inhabit, heightens the aspects of responsibility and accountability for each of us and all humanity. As has been noted, the child that comes into the world inherits from its family and its community its initial symbolic constructs that are the basis for its initial formation of its self-reflexive "I" and the world that it will perceive. As members of that community, we have a direct responsibility, not just for our own formative self-actualization but also for the cultural symbols, values, and ideas that we are creating and fostering and which will engender new generations. Are we creating value systems of openness and inclusion, trust, hope, respect, diversity, wonder, possibility, responsibility, and freedom; or are we creating value systems based on fear, exclusion, distrust, ethnocentrism, isolationism, arrogance, despair, alienation, elitism, and the abdication of responsibility that emerges from a crowd mentality? Are Jesus and his message at the heart of our personal way of viewing ourselves and our world? The core attributes of service, generosity, humility, empathy, respect, hope, and love are but a few of the demonstrated characteristics of the life of Jesus and his requirements for those who would be his disciples. Many of these attributes have been shown to be basic elements of any authentic human life. Jesus infuses these with a new level of meaning by tying them to how we as individuals and as societies discover God and bring his kingdom to this earth.

A critical aspect of humanity that not only makes humans fundamentally different than all their fellow creatures but also places them in a unique position in relationship to itself and the world in which it lives is the fact that we are self-reflexive and that this aspect of who we are has become the very basis of understanding what our most radical freedom is and what our role in our own self-actualization must be.

It is also at its core the appreciation of our role in the continued creation of our world to which we are inextricably tied. This fundamental notion of humanity has also exposed the nature of the relationship between the meanings we give to our lives, the events that fill them, and the actions that flow from them. It raises the critical fact that, whether we choose to accept it or not, we are responsible for the lives we live and the selves we are as well as the set of meanings we pass on to the next generation. In fact, this ability to choose who I am and the world that I live in is the most fundamental, critical choice we make, not once but in each and every moment.

"Arise and awake, sleeper" is the call of the abbot to the new solemnly professed monk of a Benedictine abbey. In many ways, this summons is appropriate to all of us for it is the call to each of us to grasp our lives as our own and to make of them all that we can. Wake up! Be aware of who you are! "Know yourself!" as the Greek philosopher Socrates stated as the first principal of wisdom. It is imperative that as individuals and as a society, we soberly reflect on our fundamental faculties, their powers, and their associated responsibilities. Understanding where we are actors in this drama that is our life and to be able to distinguish where we must suffer (in the most literal sense of enduring those aspects of life for which we do not have control) and how these two facets of our beings interact is an essential aspect of authentic living. Our primary freedom, as has been described, sits between these two extremes, for it is neither in our ability to control many of the events that will fill our lives nor in our ability to alter that which cannot be changed. Our freedom lies within us and is our ability to choose how we respond based on the meanings we give to these events. Thus the command to "take up your cross and follow me" (Matthew 16:24) is a command to live life, to choose the self you will be and the world you will live in and do it in a way that is authentic, responsible, generous, and life giving but always within the real constraints of the given realities which we must suffer that are not ours to control.

The Identity of the Self

Up to this point in our reflection, we have focused mostly on understanding our humanity as something we share. We have discussed our shared capabilities as well as the key aspect of human living that entails the integration of happenings, events, and givens into who we are through the willed meanings that we assign them. At this juncture we want to reflect on that which makes each of us unique, or in other words, a self.

The initial question that we must address is, "What does it means to be a self?" One of the reasons for focusing on this question is that all along we have discussed various aspects of our common humanity so that we might better understand the spirituality that rests upon it. At the end of the day each of us is called as a unique person loved into being and sustained with the hope that through their life they will make the presence of Christ a little more real to someone and thus the possibility of our redemption may be closer at hand.

Our experience of our "selves" as composed of various dimensions and capabilities is important. But without an understanding of ourselves as the unique unity that expresses these realities, we are still seriously inhibited in our self-knowledge and appreciation. Certainly each of us experiences ourselves as a physical being. We also know ourselves as thinking beings that can reason and create through imagination and understanding. We are also creatures with a rich spectrum of emotional responses to our lives. These emotions range from intense joy and wonder to heart-rending sadness, hurt, and disappointment. Each of these facets of the self brings its own unique nuances to the question of how one can truly ascertain what it means to be a unique individual or specifically to be the unique self I am. To claim that any one of these facets of the self, or even their mere combination, is adequate as a description of one's individuality would be a mistake. Once one grasps the essence of one's being, then the question of one's ability to apply one's will to who one is or who one longs to be reveals itself as a fundamental possibility.

Each of the myriad of aspects of my identity brings a nuance of understanding to who I am. Our bodily nature pinpoints us in the perspective of space and time. I experience my physical world through my body. This body places me in the now with all its givens, potentials, and limitations. It both situates me and provides a marker that enables others to know it is me with whom they are interacting. My physicality is also the vehicle through which I experience innumerable realities about myself and my world. My physical being provides opportunities to me as well as many limitations. The bodily component of my existence also is a unique process of unfolding that I experience as my own evolution from total dependence in childhood to various degrees of independence and strength that accompany my maturity. The process of aging that my body experiences inevitably turns back its initial thrust toward strength, independence, and apparent limitless possibility to the realization of my limits and a growing awareness of a natural decline and, ultimately, the reality of my death. To identify myself with my body as the essential aspect of who I am would not only diminish my human existence but certainly would be an inadequate descriptor. It is equally true that to disregard my physical being would be to seriously jeopardize any meaningful sense of how we both experience ourselves and others.

As rational beings with the capacity to think, imagine, dream, and create, we take our physical natures to new levels of experience. It would be foolish to persist in a construct of our minds and bodies as being somehow foreign to each other and distinct realities. Certainly each provides the self with unique capacities, but it does so as an integrated whole. To speak about minds without bodies (at least on the human level) is absurd. The concept of a "thinking thing," developed in the seventeenth century by René Descartes, as separate and unique from our physical natures is at best confused. That does not, however, require a material reductionist conception of human intellect. As a rational being, I have the ability to transcend my physical limitations through intellect, imagination, and thought. My actions no longer need to be just a matter of physical impulses.

Our minds imbue our lives with an ability to respond to events rather than just react, for we are able to reflect, consider, and develop our personal values that enable our ability to transcend initial non-reflective reactions. The mind is also the seat of our imagination and creativity. Cognitive creativity facilitates our ability to a degree and in ways that no other creature can. These adaptations are specifically unique because they emerge from my process of cognition. Not only does our rational nature allow each of us to think, dream, and imagine, it also is the basis of our highly developed ability to express and communicate through the creation of symbols. These symbols, whether they are words, gestures, rituals, images, or artistic manifestations, enable each person to bridge the chasm between their individual existences to a degree unimaginable by any other creature. These symbols allow us to share our ideas, feelings, experiences, and thoughts and are the basis of our ability to create nurturing and enriching communities.

Another aspect of identity as human is our capacity to experience emotions. It would be a mistake to characterize this quality of the self as a mere aspect of our mental or cognitive attributes. Most of us would agree that our emotional capacities and our cognitive capacities are very different and at times at odds. Human emotions are the unique capacity of each individual to attach his or her own being to a person, event, situation, or experience in a particular manner. This emotional component of individuality, like the mind and the body, is fully integrated into the unity of an individual's existence. In fact, human capacities such as empathy and compassion are indicative of the highly integrated aspects of our natures, for they involve our mental capacities as well as our emotional natures. Hormonal shifts as aspects of our physical natures can have significant influence on how we feel. Emotions are not necessarily merely about an event in the present. While certainly one always has feelings in the moment, the emotions I am experiencing now may be based on an event long past or the possibility of something yet to be.

Our feelings and emotions are critical to our unique natures as humans. Our emotions reveal much about how we are experiencing our lives as well as the underlying meanings we are associating with ourselves and the events of our lives. As such, they are never right or wrong. Our feelings and emotions merely express how we are experiencing a particular event, memory, thought, or happening. Combined with our memories and our intellects, these emotions can be quite complex and not always easily understood. Realizing that these signals are mere indicators of how we are experiencing something and not necessarily indicators of the "rightness" or "wrongness" of something that has happened is critical. Otherwise we can become convinced that these emotions are proper determiners of how we should assess something in our lives or how we should respond. Emotions on their own are seldom the proper indicators of good choices or what actions one should take. Our emotions certainly should be acknowledged and listened to, but never in isolation from our broader capacities.

The events or the facts of our lives are another unique aspect of one's individuality. Facts such as when a person was born and where as well as the myriad of details which surround a specific individual's existence are also real elements of his or her unique identity. While these are indisputable factors, few of us would be satisfied with a laundry list of facts as the description of our identities. The key aspect of discovering what it means to be a unique self can only be illuminated by understanding the method by which a person weaves together these facts into a life. Some of these weavings can be very deep and, dare one say, preconscious. They can be the result of messages received at too early an age to truly assess prior to their acceptance. It is for this reason that psychology has developed as a science focused on freeing us of unproductive or even destructive elements of our meanings that we have integrated without adequate understanding of their veracity.

Another aspect of our beings that is central to understand what constitutes a unique self is the human memory. Our memories facilitate the linking of one moment to the next. In addition, our memories provide each of us with the ability to experience our lives as a fluid unity as well as enabling our capacity to learn. The human memory is not merely a repository of experiences, however, but plays an even larger role in our essential identities. Our memories are not mere recorders of our life's events and our corresponding emotional reactions, be they external events or internal states. Our memories are key markers of which events we remember and how we remember them. This function of our memories means that our memories and our willed meanings interoperate in selecting which events will be retained and how they will be remembered. In this way, our memories are central to understanding the essence of the self we are. It is our memories that also are the conscious basis for our ongoing sense of self that transcends any specific moment in time and enables each of us to stitch together our remembered experiences into a single formative identity.

This discussion of memory, in fact, is the fundamental pointer to the essence of personal identity we have been striving to identify. Up to this point the elements of our identities have been common, and thus the uniqueness of the self has eluded us. As a result of reflecting on the memory, we have determined that what is stored as my memory involves two key steps. First, the identifying of an event as notable, and secondly the transforming of that event as a personal experience resulting from my willed capacity to give that event meaning. It is our personal narratives that are the essence of the self that I am. My story is the enveloping construct of my identity and thus the essence of who I am. As a story that builds upon my ongoing process of discovery, integration, and unfolding, it is a story that is constantly being reshaped, added to, and subtracted from. As such, my identity as a unique self is both real and mystery simultaneously. In this sense, each person is in the process of evolving their narrative based on their experiences as well as the meanings that shape how we internalize these into elements of our stories. Within each of our individual and unique stories are the meanings we choose as well as the interpretations of people, places, and events and our roles in them. Each of us, then, is an autobiographer, writing not with pen and paper, but with images, smells, emotions, ideas, fears, and hopes collected and influencing the next experience. The role of our wills in choosing which events to include in the story I am as well as how those events are interpreted, remembered, and placed within the larger context of my narrative as conceived thus far reveals why the capacity to create or chose particular meanings is at the heart of freedom. Freedom is the space in which humans are afforded the capability to determine the meanings that define us, our world, and our responsive. For freedom is truly the prerequisite for my capacity to participate in the self I am and will be. Without it, our ability to truly live through the struggles of our existence to determine who I shall be would be impossible.

Since it is my personal narrative that is the essence of who I am, the importance of being aware of my narrative and how it continues to operate both constructively and deleteriously in my life would seem essential. Just because my narrative is the essence of who I am does not entail that we are all as aware of our stories as one might imagine. In fact, the healing that many of us go through as we mature can be directly related to our ability to be open to and cognizant of the story that we are and operate from. The question of how we can become more aware of our personal narratives as the vital source of our identities and as the foundations of how we experience our lives and our selves is critical. From what we have established thus far, it is imperative that we grasp both the fluid nature of these narratives and thus our ability to alter them as we become more in possession of the key elements that shape our stories.

There are many methods of becoming more aware of the stories that each of us is. Meditation and self-reflection are the exercises that many use to get in touch with the richness of their own personal stories. Many people see psychiatrists or psychologists for this purpose. Our ability to own who we are at any point in our lives requires that we truly appreciate the narrative that we live under as the essence of our individual identity. As has been discussed in great length, the meanings we have given to the happenings of our lives are critical elements of our personal narratives and must be brought forth to ensure that our personal stories and their many chapters are not inhibiting us from the rich and full lives we desire and deserve. For these narratives are the basis of how we experience ourselves and our world. To the degree that we find our lives empty, meaningless, unfulfilled, or ourselves limited in connecting with others in constructive and nurturing ways will have a direct link with the narrative under which we are living. Authentic, mature assessments of these narratives are critical as we age and seek to own who we are, who we have been, and who we wish to be. Every person has aspects of their narratives that require exposition and re-appropriation. This is the process of self-actualization, self-healing, and forgiveness of self and others that is necessary as a part of our path to self-love.

The story which is the core of any individual is the meaning given to the enormous number of events that make up his or her existence.

The story of who I am is the reality of who I am. Previously, the dimensions of time have been emphasized as essential to identity. Stories or narratives, by their very construct, are the methods used to give unity, sense, and flow to events, history, and even more importantly, to the meanings that shape our identities. Most of us have had lives filled with joy and pain. The suffering and thrills of existence are not what make me different from you. What establishes one's individuality is what we choose to highlight from mere incidents into significant aspects of our personal narratives, which unifies our pasts into fundamentally unique selves that reflect these meanings in our ways of being in the present.

The process of owning one's narrative as the most essential act of personal integrity is often not easy. It requires that each of us accepts our active participation in our individual identities. It requires humility and strength, for each of us must face the divergence between the selves we actually are and the selves we often try to convince ourselves and others that we are. It is the greatest gift of our lives that what has been is only ephemeral, written, as it were, in smoke and always capable of being transformed by our ability to re-appropriate the past in a manner that enables me to grow beyond it and from it. For Christians, the formative integration of the message of Jesus and the receptivity of the Spirit that accompanies one's personal conversion is the second birth that Christ spoke of. It is in many respects our personal resurrection from our previous narratives to a transformed story based on the principles, values, and meanings espoused by Jesus and carried in the truth of the Spirit, which transforms our limited existence to the fullness of life. It requires that each of us face our own Gethsemanes, where the truth of who we are and have been can be exposed, healed, and re-appropriated into a revised narrative. This process takes significant self-honesty, humility, and the ability to forgive one's self as well as others.

A necessary skill required for us to be open to this self-possession and the authentic life that can spring from it is our ability to listen.

A key skill necessary for becoming aware of our own stories, and thus our increased ability to truly be open to the stories of others, is dependent on our continued capacity to listen. Listening is not easy. It is not merely taking in the sounds that surround us at each instant of our lives. Mature listening is another fundamental act of will. It is the choice to focus on myself or another and to shut out the prattle that can consume us. Reactive listening is something we all do as a matter of survival. It is a vague awareness that keeps us attuned to danger or opportunity. The listening being described here is not this instinctual awareness. The listening being advocated here is an act of the will to give my attention to another for the specific purpose of taking in and being open to another. It is a focusing of my internal and external ear to a particular object and thus it is an act of my will. This kind of listening shuts out the noise that often seeks to avoid such receptivity.

Listening is as critical a skill but not adequate in and of itself. In fact, if we have yet to discover how to listen to our internal selves, it is highly unlikely we really have the capacity to listen to others. Listening is the first step toward self-knowledge, healing, and loving. It is only within this context that an individual can make the step from listening to hearing. Listening makes us aware and disposes us to the possibility of hearing. Hearing requires listening and builds on the attentiveness that listening makes possible.

Hearing requires that we have mastered the art of listening. As a second step, it also requires the individual will. When we actually hear ourselves or another, we allow the other to be the true focus. We remove our ego as the filter through which our hearing occurs. This posture is thus one of empathy and compassion. In hearing another, I am seeking to understand his or her world and his or her experiences as he or she does, without judgment. Hearing is essential in the transformation we spoke of above that is the outcome of reassessing critical aspects of our stories that have held us back. Truly allowing oneself to hear another is an act of generosity, courage, hope, and faith. In hearing, we let down our defenses and have the courage to let the other speak without consideration of the effect on the self. This can be very difficult when two people are experiencing interpersonal difficulties.

In the act of focusing my hearing on myself, I must have the courage to face something unpleasant in myself, which requires a conscious displacement of my ego with its judgments and assessments from the center of my ability to hear. Without this displacement, I may be prone to justify or become overly harsh in my personal assessments. Neither is very helpful. True hearing is letting myself or the other be accepted and respected as in unfinished, incomplete, and thus capable of startling me. Judgments are not helpful and belie a lack of complete openness. Letting the other expose how they feel and how they experience something without our having to correct or judge is an important indicator of just how effective we are as individuals seeking to hear ourselves and the other. Being able to hear where one may have hurt another or how one's behavior can affect another is a two-sided gift. It enables the hearer to become aware and see an aspect of themselves that they may have been unaware of. It also allows the sharer to let go of a weight that may have been keeping two friends apart or colleagues estranged. Hearing is not something we should do only with other people. We should continually attempt to keep an ear cocked to our inner selves. Over time, we can become more in tune to our postures, our inner turmoil, and the messages that emerge from them as we live our lives. Without the ability to listen and hear, it is hard to imagine how we can truly live up to the command of the "Our Father," which is "to forgive us our trespasses as we forgive those who trespass against us."

Egocentric listening is grasping and judgmental. It is less about hearing and more about assessing. As Christians, we are asked to avoid judgment, for it is an act of disruption within the community. Instead, we are asked to listen and hear our brothers and sisters and in our awareness of our common humility and weakness to shore one another up. By so doing, we create a silence in which we have both the courage and gentleness to hear our stories as we have formed them. We are placed in the context of self-discovery, joy, humility, and forgiveness. Our world is not a natural habitat for such dwelling. Our ability to fill every moment with noise, assessments, external benchmarks, and continued marching forward, deaf to the richness of who we are and who we can be, is a force to be reckoned with. The only method proven as effective across creeds, cultures, and times has been the choice to create the space to rediscover ourselves, our neighbors, and our vocations through the creation of the practice of listening. This time set aside is the willed generous act of developing the lost skill of stillness, openness, and resting in God's merciful hands. There are thousands of books in almost all traditions written over the centuries about this critical practice and its foundation for hearing the truth of ourselves, our world, and others.

Developing a consciousness that is awake to our inner narrative and that is deepening in its appreciation of it and its complexity is not something that can be achieved without effort. In our world of constant noise, endless activity, and a basic orientation toward the self as defined by externals, it requires first an awareness of what it means to be a self and then the desire to know the self I am. There are two major methods for self-knowledge that are at the heart of the approach offered. While these approaches may seem antithetical, they are truly complementary. In fact, one without the other calls into question the effectiveness of the whole.

The first of the two methods for discovering the self is through the process of living, which is the continual process of giving myself away. This may sound trite, but it is anything but. Experience is the first path to self-discovery and knowledge. By living life to its full and being open to new experiences as well as the everyday, an individual's underlying narrative will manifest itself. As this narrative is the very foundation for how we experience our world, people, situations, and things, these experiences will offer significant clues into the natures of our underlying identities. In order to be able to hear these clues, however, one must make use of the second method, which has already been alluded to but now is placed within its complete context. This second facet of self-discovery is continuous self-realization through the practice of appropriate silence, thoughtfulness, and honest self-assessments. It is only with the development of an internal attention that the messages that life and experience will offer to us will be provided the necessary space to be heard. The space required for the discovery of our pre-reflective narratives is at the heart of our ability both to know ourselves and our capacity to be responsible for the selves we are.

Self-narratives are neither good nor bad, but they can be life affirming or severely limiting of personal fulfillment and peace. Understanding our personal stories as a source of our strengths as well as our weaknesses is essential to discovering our capacity to be free and to be able to transcend the pre-reflective responses that we have come to discover are patterns born of unresolved aspects of our personal stories. Allowing our personal narratives to float to the surface of our consciousness is an act of courage as well as will. It often requires significant personal fortitude and honesty as we face aspects of ourselves that may be humbling or even painful.

As Christians, we profess a desire to continue to assess our personal narratives in light of the narrative of Jesus and the apostles. Through ongoing contemplation on his story and on the meaning of that story for our own narratives, we commit ourselves to an ongoing dialogue between the gospels and our unfolding selves. Personal narratives shape our values, which are the source of the principles that define us. As adults, we have the capacity to actively participate in the narratives we are and also to choose what influences will be formative of them. As Christians, we are called to open our narratives to these formative influences through ritual, prayer, and reading, as well as through ongoing acts of charity. Once again, our wills are key in choosing: first, to become more conscious of our own narrative; second, to become more responsible for its formation and reformation; and third, to determine what the formative influences of the selves we are shall be on our families, coworkers, and neighbors. To the degree that we do not expose ourselves thoughtfully and prayerfully to the narrative that is Jesus's life, we cannot hope or claim to be serious in our desire to be one of his followers.

Reading about the great men and women who have lived heroic and meaningful lives, regardless of their faith traditions, is a wonderful way to learn about the power and the freedom of our wills to own our stories and to expand our existence for the greater glory of our God. There is an old saying. If you want to know a person, look at who they associate with. I believe it would be better said that if you want to know a person, notice what they read, notice if and how they listen, notice how they spend their time and how self-possessed they appear in bad times as well as good. See if they have the capacity to dwell. By dwell I mean their ability to sit with uncertainty and to truly opine on the alternatives that are possible before choosing to act. What do they hear, or (probably easier to discover) what do they listen to?

Who we are is a process of creation which only stops when we do. This cessation can be by physical death or willed death. Our consistent mantra has been that authenticity evokes authenticity. We will fulfill Jesus' commitment that he came that we might have life and have it more abundantly by dedicating ourselves to own our lives and thereby drawing others deeper into their own. We should all practice the ancient non-religion-based tradition of dwelling. We should all have the courage to determine what things may stand between us and the selves we long for and remove them. Holy men and women are not all poor or Christian, but they all have had the courage to clear out the garbage that has made each of them believe they are either in control of life or victims of life. The silence that is truly holy is seldom assertive. First and foremost, it has at its center not the grasping ego and its desires, but truth, beauty, love, and the stillness that these evoke. Only when we are willing to will our center, or ego, to the "Other," can we truly listen—to ourselves and those around us—authentically and not through our own self-centered egos.

Jesus' life was filled with noise. His public ministry was characterized by thousands thronging "like sheep without a shepherd" (Matthew 9:36). At every corner, there were those who waited with traps to ensnare him. It seemed at times that even those closest to him did not comprehend the most basic parts of what he was trying to convey. What allowed this man to stay focused? What consistently made him able to hear what others seemed deaf to and to have the energy and generosity to respond? The gospels are replete with the answer. He went off by himself to be with his Father and to pray. Even Jesus, who many claim as both man and God, grasped the essential need to dwell and to listen as yet another act of his generous will. Can we really expect to be his true followers without being true to this same call?

The Eternal Dance of the "I" and the Other

An essential element in understanding the self is in understanding its origins, its process of unfolding. Eric Fromm, a famous psychologist, spent significant effort describing this process in *The Art of Loving*. Fromm rightly linked the development of the self with the realization of the non-self, or other. The first such primal experience is in the separation of the infant from the mother at birth. Fromm labeled this experience as our first realization of *separateness*. Separateness is a technical term used by Fromm to describe not just this first primal experience but also the experiences that can apply throughout our lives and in terms of which we can assess our growth via how we respond to this experience as the essential defining element between what Fromm will define as an authentic interaction model and self-construct and an inauthentic one. This dynamic of the relationship between our ability to embrace our separateness and thus our individuality, as well as our healthy experience of individuation that is described as "aloneness," are key to our growth and actualization. Fromm's contention is that this dialectic of the self and the other continues as we continue to mature. The more developed our sense of self, the more developed and nuanced will be its complement and vice versa.

Fromm appreciates, however, the primitive desire of humanity to rediscover the unity that existed prior to the separateness of individuation. This desire for unity is fueled by our need to rediscover the completeness that was ours prior to our first primitive experience of separateness. This desire is neither negative nor positive in and of itself. It functions to drive the individual to engage his or her world (i.e., persons, situations, and things) as the proper method of self-discovery and authentic love. This is an essential step in becoming a self-reflexive "I." The alternative to this openness to and interaction with the other is radical alienation and isolation and thus the profound experience of separateness. Separateness, which is the negative experience of the primitive self, entails a terrifying sense of loss. Fromm sees this primal experience of separateness as the motivating energy that continues to drive the relationship between the "I" and the "other." It is the basic thrust that enables the individual to overcome the fear associated with reaching out and the subsequent undetermined outcomes. For Fromm, the individual continues through life to fill the void of separateness by creating relationships with the other. It is the response of the individual to this innate drive outward and the corresponding fear of the potential uncontrollable outcomes coupled with our desire to control any potential negative experiences of life that are essential in understanding the pitfalls in this process of maturation.

In the creation myth of the Old Testament, we see the same individual need for others as the prerequisite of personal unfolding as well as the essential method for circumventing the paralyzing experience of isolation and loneliness. The biblical passage that specifically addresses this need occurs after God has created the earth and all its creatures, including Adam. The myth relates that God discovers that his first human creature, Adam, is despondent. Within the context of this myth, God realized that Adam required an other that was equal to him in stature and with whom he could share his life, and so God made Eve. The myth has Eve being constructed from Adam's rib. Eve is thus flesh of his flesh. Eve is neither second nor derivative, but of the same matter and spirit. It is very significant that God does not go back to the dust of the earth to create Eve but constructs Eve from Adam himself. They are therefore one nature.

So according to this myth, not only did Adam now have a companion, but more importantly, Adam had a true soul mate. We know, however, that this is not enough. Certainly having other people in our world and having the ability to find individuals that we love and with whom we can share our lives are important aspects of our ability to grow as selves and are essential in dealing with the separateness that we all have experienced, but the availability of others does not guarantee that the individual will truly engage with the other. Our fear of rejection, being perceived as undesirable, or unable to live up to the expectations of others is a significant factor in the dynamics of truly engaging the world, people, and situations.

Fromm highlighted the fact that dealing with separateness is universal; how we deal with it is not. There are two modes that can describe the method by which an individual interacts with the world. These two modes describe the degree to which an individual is truly engaging reality. One is characterized by openness, trust, and a willingness to be surprised by life as well as a willingness to be hurt. The other mode may appear to be equally engaged with life, but this engagement is severely limited by fear, a lack of trust; a need, therefore, to control and manipulate life as a method of self-protection. The former orientation to life is described by Fromm as an authentic stance toward the world. The latter is characterized as an inauthentic disposition. These responses are always descriptive of how the self stands in relationship to the other.

Authentic ways of standing in the presence of the other require that we accept the other as truly outside our ability to control, inherently individual and unique, and indeed a mystery to be discovered and cherished in his or her otherness. This acceptance of the other as independent of me, and thus in some sense foreign, entails that I be willing to take a risk in the act of self-disclosure, for I cannot know or determine the other's response. It also means that the self must accept the fact that it is by its nature incomplete and unique and will always be so. These two dimensions result in the fact that no other person can or will ever be able to eradicate my individuality and aloneness. Fromm asserts that the other and the self can share and love, but no matter how much one person loves another, the other can never bridge the basic gulf of individuality.

This experience is an affirmation that each of us is a fundamentally unique person with our own individual identities, histories, abilities, strengths, fears, and weaknesses. We should greet the world with an orientation to embrace it on multiple levels—intellectually, emotionally, and psychologically. At the same time, we also want from the world, especially people, to be desired, accepted, respected, and acknowledged. Our many needs depend on the situation, the particular person, and our specific psycho-historical constitution. All of this is quite normal. It is when the self is in a state of desperation for control and moves from an embracing posture to a grasping and clutching mode that the distortions associated with a need to control take over.

It is the playing out of this tension between the self and the other that affords each of us the opportunity to create, as an act of will, authentic or inauthentic relationships. Inauthenticity is demonstrated by an inherent desire to eradicate the primal experience of separateness from which Fromm has described as essential to the proper development of the individual. It is the need to remove that which makes the individual feel "separate from." It is a fleeing from our experience of individuation. It is the desire to be either subsumed in the other or to obliterate the experience of the other as different from ourselves.

Separateness can also be manifest in a psychological distancing of the self from the world in order to achieve the same experience of pseudo-wholeness that is characteristic of inauthenticity. It is the denial of the other as a unique subject and the attempt to make him or her the extension of another. Whatever form it takes, it is the individual's attempt to experience a level of completeness that is not possible in this life. This tendency toward eradication of the other as the confused method of experiencing unity is a compelling temptation. It is not merely associated with youth or immaturity but can manifest itself throughout one's life. The discipline associated with our continued ability to be comfortable with our vulnerability, our aloneness, and to embrace our subjectivity as well as that of others requires ongoing effort. Inauthentic existence is often exhausting for those who attempt to live in denial of the realities of life by attempting to control what cannot be controlled. For those desperately attempting to clutch onto others, situations, and themselves, life can become a downward spiral of manipulation, lies, and disappointments. Even when it appears to be succeeding, this life of pseudo-unity can never deliver its false promise. The world with all its riches cannot replace the wonder and mystery that is at the core of each person's soul. No matter how wonderful another person may be, he can never expunge the individual that I am.

This inherent desire to control is basic to humanity and demonstrable throughout our history. This innate need is certainly understandable. Whether one refers to it as fate, cause and effect, or the outcome of mercurial deities, the fact is that life is both unpredictable, and at times, cruel. Awful things happen to good people, and awful people often seem to slide through the vicissitudes of life. This apparent randomness of events is hard to deal with for the most mature of us. It is, however, our ability to convince ourselves that we can control reality which often prevents the self from blossoming forth. Examples of inappropriate methods of dealing with life's otherness can be seen in individuals who define themselves as victims and blame their situations on others or fate. They are abdicating their capability to participate in life via our basic freedom, as opposed to being controlled by the events that all people must deal with. How we choose to see our lives and our ability to cast meanings that enable our continued engagement of life are critical to authentic living. Otherwise we will find ourselves buffeted by the winds of fortune and misfortune. If we do not choose this mode of existence, we will have tossed away our rudder so that we do not have to accept responsibility for who we are or how we have responded to life. Often, we abdicate our freedom so as not to face the cost of our choices or inactions.

At the core of each self is a will, our ability to choose. These choices are real and often difficult because they involve situations and events whose outcomes we cannot determine. The authentic self is no less afraid, vulnerable, or able to be hurt than the inauthentic person. The difference is that the inauthentic individual refuses to engage the world as it is and to exercise his or her will regardless of the external happenings that life may throw at him or her. Authenticity takes a radically different posture toward life. The authentic individual perceives his or her life and the lives of others as a gift.

Our interaction with life comes from our internal sense of self and expresses itself in our willingness to be present, exposed, and generous with what life offers us. This personal generosity of spirit is the lived courage called forth in Christ's admonition to "take up your cross and follow me" (Matthew 16:24–25). It is also at the core of the call to give up one's life in order that one may find it. The human spirit is shaped in hardship. Our characters are molded by our willed responses to what we cannot control. It is the confrontation of true human freedom with liberty that is at the heart of the Christian struggle. Christianity was born on a cross that was neither just nor deserved. The heart of the Christian message was announced to each of us in the final words of the one who bore humanity's worst cruelties and injustice when he cried out, "Father forgive them" (Luke 23:24). There is no greater example of the triumph of human freedom over the limitations and illusions of liberty.

In order to achieve this degree of personal authenticity and freedom, one must begin by accepting the aloneness that is at the core of the experience of individuality. This aloneness is not an acceptance of loneliness, which is the result of removing oneself from others, as well as firmly ensconcing our egos at the center of reality. Aloneness is the proper realization of our individuality. This aloneness never requires that the individual be lonely. In fact, quite to the contrary, it demands that each of us reach out to life and to others and give ourselves away. In the Buddhist tradition, this concept of finding peace through self-offering is at the heart of the path of dharma. Buddhism has grasped and promulgated for centuries that the source of all suffering is not in my offering of myself to the other, but in the ego as the misplaced center of my being. Healthy aloneness does require, however, the acceptance that no other individual will ever be able to take away my fundamental individuality. It requires that the other, as other, must be accepted and respected as such. The other, like myself, must be understood as fundamentally unique and therefore as his own individual self. Any expectation that the other will obliterate my experience of aloneness or separateness is misguided. It is for this reason that inauthentic relationships are not capable of expressing the fullness of love, for love requires two individuals who are willing to act with generosity by sharing themselves with each other.

The pinnacle of authentic interactions is expressed when the self chooses to offer itself for the good of the other. It means truly realizing that the other is not merely an extension of me, my needs, and my ways of perceiving reality. Inauthenticity has at its core the belief that the other can be the hoped-for missing piece that will fill the experience of internal emptiness that is part of being a mature individual. Infatuation is an extreme example of this kind of inauthentic love. A reasonable question one might ask is, if my sense of "I," or my ego, is not to be at the core of the self, what is? The answer is for the Christian, Christ. For the Buddhist, it may be the other. But to truly claim to be a follower or disciple of Jesus is to strive to see the world from the perspective of God. The actual ability to see from God's perspective is not highly probable; it is the striving that is essential. When we open up to the other, it is this perspective that allows us to transcend our all-too-human reactions based on appearance, prejudice, or the callousness that can build up around our hearts over time.

This ability to accept the other as other is no mean feat. It is not merely something we contend with in infancy, childhood, or adolescence. There are, however, specific points in human development at which this struggle can be very much at the surface. The reason infatuation is so often experienced in youth is that the developing individual is still in its formative stage, and the immature longing of the emerging self to discover someone who can take away his or her ever-increasing experiences of aloneness (whether truly conscious or not) is so intensified because adolescence is the in-between state of the self as defined by others and the emerging self-defining itself. It is for this reason that these first love experiences, often experienced in our mid- to late teens and early twenties, can be so very potent and potentially dangerous. Not only is the emerging self desperately seeking to feel desirable, understood, and unique, but at the same time it is still longing once again to feel completed by someone else.

Infatuation, as an inauthentic response to the other, is the desire to lose oneself in the other. Authenticity is the desire to find oneself by giving oneself to the other. It is a shame that most of us carry the image of human birth around in our minds as something that happens in a hospital room at the end of a term of pregnancy. This notion that we are born finished creates unrealistic and stressful expectations in both the adults who deal with children and the parents who at times feel on storm-tossed seas, never quite sure if or when dry land will bring them and their child home safe and sound.

Maybe some of the wrenching escapades that have been so common across loving and caring families would be less heightened if the expectation of completeness were not quite so prevalent.

Up to now, much time has been spent focusing on the other from the perspective of the self. This might give one the impression that the other is a mere passive element in the world. This would certainly be a significant error, for the "Other" plays much more than a passive role in life. The other is, as we have noted, an outcome of our willed meanings, and yet, paradoxically the "Other" is the reality that continually evokes each of us to greater awareness of what is and not what we may like to tell ourselves. Life, reality, the world, God (as the all-encompassing Other), and the many individuals we come in contact with constantly impose themselves on us, consistently challenging our often incomplete, narrow, inaccurate, stilted, warped, self-serving views. The other, as our first experience of the transcendent (that which exists beyond me), will always act as a mirror to the self that I am, calling me to see myself as I am and not as I would like to be.

The world as other continuously attempts to evoke authenticity. The paradox should be apparent. From the perspective of the self, the world is a creative act of the willed meanings of the self-reflexive "I," and yet the world exists as something truly other. This paradox is also evident in that I really exist as a unique person, yet my identity is the result of how I give meaning to who I am. In short, therefore, the world is both truly other and independent of me, and at the same time shaped by not only me, but by all who perceive and interact with it in the act of co-creation. The world, in people, situations, and things is continually reflecting reality back to each of us. In many respects, the world is more than just the stage of Shakespeare's players who "strut and fret." It is a corrective mirror in which humanity is offered an honest view, if we have but the courage to attend.

Lest the irony escape us, this world has been described as having two dimensions: an objective dimension, which is not ours to know but is the object of God's creative genius, and the world that each of us experiences, which is a mixture of God's objective world and our co-creative wills and the worlds they expose to each of us. The degree to which our experiences of this world are distorted is indeed a factor of our authentic or inauthentic life choices. This reality of the otherness of the world is another example of the human experience of mystery. This mystery is the acknowledgement that no one can grasp the world in its pure objectivity. As with our experiences of ourselves, which we have already shown also entail mystery, we are once again confronting the ineffable as both a real and a rational aspect of human experience. It is not just a matter of having the time to figure it out or being able to get an adequate amount of data; it is the coming face to face with the unknowable. It is this touching of the limits of our capacities and our possibilities that makes this experience for many not just terrifying but even infuriating and completely unacceptable.

Our experiences with other persons are not somehow different in kind from our experiences of the world. No matter how many years one may know another individual the mystery of the other will never be plumbed. The other is not, nor ever will be, a solvable problem. Mystery is thus not an unnatural concept applied for convenience; rather it is a description of our existential realities and our appreciation of ourselves as unfolding processes. As human beings, we are always in process or, said another way, emerging in relationship to the other (our world). More technically stated, our identities are a dialectical construct whose beings are defined in the tension between the self and the other. This tension is both constitutive and creative. It involves both the possibility of deception and the hope of correction. It is, however, at its most fundamental an action of the free will, for it entails insight, choice, and the continual opportunity for discovery and disclosure.

The basis of this corrective hope is the true otherness of the world that, while always ineffable in its totality, is available as fundamentally real, external, approachable, and independent of my will for its being. It is this otherness in all its varied manifestations that calls each person to respond in each moment of life. Humanity's fundamental orientation of consciousness toward the world as both the context in which each individual will discover and create him or herself and then continuously correct that creation through interaction with that world reinforces again that humanity and the world are interlocked and interdependent creations. It also reaffirms that the proper orientation of life is in the opening up of the human spirit through continual engagement with life. This, we will see, requires a posture of generosity, trust, and faith.

The above provides our first experiential description of the transcendent in human life. It describes our experience of the fundamental trajectory of the human spirit or consciousness toward the other that is the very basis for the discovery of the self. Self-actualization through authentic relationships is an orientation toward living in that it is never an achievable acquisition of the other, but rather an orientation toward the other. In fact, both the other and the self remain permanently ineffable and thus mysteries to be cherished. The nature of this mystery is in part defined by the non-static nature of both the self and the other. This directional nature of the self's consciousness toward the other as a fundamental element in the self's own creative process is the first-order definition of the transcendent within humanity. As such, transcendence as we are defining it is not an incidental aspect of our experience; it is in fact an essential element of our ability to exist as humans. Without this experience of our own transcendence as directionally orienting each of us to what is the object of our consciousness, the self would not be discoverable, for the Other would not be there drawing us forward into being and self-actualization.

It is critical that we grasp that neither mystery nor transcendence are thus foreign, contrived constructs, but rather actual dimensions of our human experience. The importance of this appreciation is essential if we are to more fully grasp another dimension of transcendence, which is the relationship between what Martin Buber called the "I and Thou." For this "I-Thou" relationship is like the story attributed to the ancients of a worm that once looked heavenward and, seeing a butterfly, mused to itself, "You'd never get me in one of those things." Buber's "I and Thou" is the relationship between the self and God, which should not be thought of as foreign or fanciful, for it mirrors our own natural experience. As the truly transcendent Other, God is the supreme ineffable that beckons each of us as the author, lover, master, and end of our being. While the specific approach so far has certainly focused on our experiences as persons in interaction with other persons, things, and situations, this experiential model is not fundamentally inconsistent with how we can or must experience our relationships with God. Just as we are fundamentally mysteries to ourselves and must always remain so and be cherished as such, so must be our appreciation, wonder, and awe of the divine. This realization that the characteristics of our experience of the divine should not be thought of as foreign to human experience but rather as an extension of the true nature of how we stand in relationship to each other and ourselves is pivotal.

The anthropology and cosmology presented here consistently posits a view of creation that, rather than being in opposition to the divine, is set in relationship with the divine. It is the view of the "Other," who is sacred and redemptive. It is a relationship which is always beckoning and wooing the beloved from the deepest recesses of our beings. "As a hart longs for flowing streams, so longs my soul for thee, O God. My soul thirsts for God, for the living God. When shall I come and behold the face of God? My tears have been my food day and night, while men say to me continually, 'Where is your God?'" (Psalm 42:1–3). Even the notion of the world as a mirror that not only reflects back to us who we are, but is a mechanism for self-construction and correction as it presents to us our own distortions has its theological corollary in the relation between God the Father and Christ, the second person of the Trinity, in the medieval speculum metaphor.

This image of a mirror is an ancient one. In the Middle Ages, theologians often used the metaphor of the *speculum* (Latin for mirror) as the image for understanding the relationship between God and Christ. This metaphor is a depiction of the back of the head of God looking into a mirror and the face of Christ displayed within the mirror in full view. Here a visual image is used between the first and second persons of the Trinity. The mirror in this model is perfect and thus replicates the archetype as an image without any distortion. Typically, this relationship is described, as in the Gospel of St. John, as that between God who speaks and Christ, the perfect expression; or, as the Greeks thought of it, Christ the Logos (Word) of God. In the speculum metaphor, however, we see a harkening back to the *imago Dei* concept of the Old Testament. The difference, when the metaphor is a visual model depicting the relationship between God and Christ, is that it is no longer ad imago Dei (to or toward the image of God) but in imagem Dei (in the image of God as a necessary outcome); and thus it discards the notion of unrealized potential because it is then necessarily irrelevant, for truly Christ is the perfect image of the Father. It is, however, very significant that this same metaphor is brought forth from Genesis to an understanding of the relationship between Christ, the Second Person of the Trinity, and the Father. By so doing, the medieval theologians are clearly aligning the relationship between humanity as the potential image of God and Christ as the actual image of God. Thus humanity and Creator are again being aligned as not incongruous, but rather the Creator is being portrayed as humanity fully actualized, as in the person of Jesus.

This *speculum* metaphor enables a far more mature concept of the final judgment than has been proliferated down through the ages. It fosters a model of the human person as a real partner in his or her own individual creation as well as his or her subsequent role in their personal salvation. The notion of humanity as simultaneously both creature and co-creator of the self sets the very stage on which our wills are positioned as the central character in the drama of our chosen lives. Who I am is, in the final analysis, the result of a multitude of choices—some blithely made with a modicum of awareness and some wrenched from my very core, but all of these choices stitched together constitute who I am. Final judgment within this metaphorical context is not the exterior verdict handed down by a God who is more in the likeness of a moral accountant than the author and sustainer of our lives. In this metaphorical model, based on humanity as a true actor in its own and its world's salvation, final judgment is the ultimate facing of each of us as we were conceived in the mind of God from all eternity versus the actual person which each of us has created through a lifetime of choices.

What is essential to understand in this metaphor is that, at the moment when each of us faces our God, we shall face ourselves as he created us to be, and to the degree that there is recognition, there is a coming home, a restful reception of a long traveled friend or salvation. To the degree that we experience estrangement and alienation from ourselves (and thus from God), there is true, complete and inconsolable alienation, isolation, and anguish. In this metaphor of archetype and image, there is no external wrath poured out upon the complex life choices each human must make and live with. A life led through repeated acts of willed selfishness and the shutting out of the world and its calls for self-giving as well as life's continued offering of personal course corrections when we have deviated from our authentic paths, will yield a realization of our radical alienation from ourselves. What greater agony can one imagine than the loss of one's self as expressed in this metaphor? On the other hand, how incomprehensible will be the peace and joy that will accompany our final destination of unity associated with seeing and knowing ourselves within the unique image of ourselves in God?

Within the speculum framework, the "judgment" which each of us must face at the end of our lives on this earth is the facing of who we have willed into existence in juxtaposition with who God offered us to be. It is the facing of how our co-creative capacity has molded our actual identity that is our self-judgment. This realization of who we have actually become in juxtaposition with the full capacities of who we might have been will be our final moment of truth.

A unique concept of the human person has been expounded herein that began with an appreciation of humanity's being a creature of this world and yet capable of transcending its constraints like no other creature through its will and its freedom, which are intimately linked. The relationship between the individual and the world, now defined in a broader sense of persons, places, situations, and things, is also the grounding through which each person discovers him or herself and creates who he or she will be and the world in which he or she will live. Paradoxically, while humans can be co-creative with their experiential selves and worlds, including other people, we can never obliterate the otherness and mystery of the real other that is there despite its ineffability. These "others" will always serve as corrective agents to each of our distortions and mirror back to us, if we have the courage to attend, the selves we are as opposed to the selves we may want to believe we are.

This is a view of the human person as radically free, responsible, and accountable both individually and, by extension, as a society. We are social creatures that cannot exist and develop outside a communal construct. In fact, we are beings that truly discover ourselves in the process of interacting with our world, i.e., in giving ourselves away. Each of us is inherently a being in time that has broken the chains of instinct as the sole determinants of action through the development of symbols and culture that are the natural artifacts of our historicity (Gordon Kaufman, *In The Face of Mystery*). This concept of mystery, rather than being an escape clause for metaphysicians and theologians, has been demonstrated to be a fundamental facet of our experience of our world and ourselves. This same mystery also characterizes our basic stance toward our God, hopefully no longer as something foreign and peculiar to the "faith" game but rather as an extension of something we now know is experientially quite natural to our everyday reality.

Within the dynamic of the self and the other, there must develop a relationship of mutual respect, forbearance, and love. It is characterized by a letting be. It is counter to the grasping, egocentric, controlling orientation that is so common in our world today. This orientation is not just to the other as other people, but also to our selves, who must take on multiple roles in this complex world. Many of us are parents, lovers, bosses, colleagues, competitors, and on and on. In our desire to ensure that these roles are not splintered selves but one integrated self expressing common values in multiple arenas, it is critical that the energy that drives each of these roles be honestly assessed to ensure it truly is an expression of one undivided self. This process begins from a profound appreciation of our own values, values not borrowed or dependent on anyone, but inherently ours.

From a Christian perspective, this belief is fostered from the firm acceptance that you have been loved first by God. This love created you, sustains you, and calls you to fuller life every day. It is only when one truly accepts one's own value, wonder, and giftedness that the value, wonder, and giftedness of the other can be ever truly appreciated. Empathy and compassion, which are at the heart of any social fabric, have their source in the individual experience of being loved, of the experience of the gift of life, of the awareness that what I have and the opportunities I have been given I have not always deserved. It is the acknowledgement that there are smarter people out there who are not as well off, there are better people who are struggling more than I am, and therefore true human connectedness comes from the admitting that what separates us is less important than what makes us the same. It is this which allows for empathy, not judgment; compassion, not disgust. It is the essential prerequisite for letting one's world get larger, not smaller. The first step in loving someone is seeing them. It is within this space that the Paraclete—literally "the one who walks along side"—is let in to speak to us and to guide us as the harbinger of peace, truth, and love.

Love—What Does It Mean Within the Context of the "Will"?

The human will has now been given its proper place within the context of our existence. The challenge at this point is to clarify what love is as opposed to how love is often portrayed in our modern lives. Understanding more precisely the nature of what is entailed in the meaning of love and its relationship to our wills is an essential aspect of achieving this goal. The very foundation of the will to love is that there is not only a relationship between love and our capacity to will, but that this relationship is both a necessary and sufficient condition for love. In short, where there is no capacity for a free act of the will, there is also no potential for love.

Gaining clarity around the concept of love first requires that the pretenders to love be exposed as such and that their limitations be clearly understood. So much of what we hear in the lyrics of love songs or view through motion pictures, novels, and almost any media stresses aspects of love that are truly wonderful but not essential. As with our discussion of freedom and liberty, love needs to be juxtaposed with liking as our method of exposing love's essence. Love, as with any other complex human reality, has many dimensions. Western culture's distortion of love is in the overemphasizing of certain attributes of our experiences when we initially encounter one of the most profound experiences of love, romantic love. Certainly the 1960s and Hollywood have done much to distort and confuse the deeper and more multi-textured meaning of love. In opposition to these tremendous forces within our society that drive us to often distorted views of love stands the life of Jesus as the perfect expression of the essence of love both in word and deed. The life of Jesus of Nazareth is a *tour de force* of love. It is not just what Jesus said about love that makes his life so important to this topic. It is in the actual living of his life expounded in the Gospels that provides the opportunity to grasp love's essential nature.

Being a Christian and not being very clear on what love is and what role it has in one's life is more than mere irony. It is certainly one of the greatest challenges of Christianity today to separate ourselves from the distortions of love that prevail so that we can recommit ourselves, no matter what our denomination, to the radical call to love that Jesus demanded of anyone who wished to follow in his footsteps. In order for this to happen, each of us must become reacquainted with the truth of love, and most specifically for Christians, how it imbued the life of Jesus. I fear that this same process may yet be required for many of the other creeds that have up to now been less poisoned by modern distortions. This reality is based on the fact that most (I would say all except I have not studied every faith tradition) religions and the spiritualities that they seek to express are centered on love. The bloodless Christianity devoid of human life and will is not worthy of the moniker "Christian" and threatens to make irrelevant what is at the center of our personal and cultural survival, the transformative and salvific participation within the nature of human love.

In modern languages, especially English, we can love almost anything: people, food, animals, the job our painter did on the house, our haircut—you name it. Love in our vernacular is almost always associated with a very positive feeling or an emotion. When coupled with romance, it is often an extreme emotion but an emotion nonetheless. This view of love based on feelings is not only misconceived but inherently problematic in its influence on our abilities to create long-term, meaningful relationships, as well as families, in whatever form they might take. As we have already noted, the emotional aspects of our human existence are critical in allowing us to be fully present to the realities of our existence. We have already noted that they are temporal, neither right nor wrong, and often realities to which we are passive.

Like any complex reality, love involves many elements of our nature. To say that love does not involve emotions or feelings would certainly be naïve. It is important, though, to discern the role of emotions and feelings within the nature of love. To do this more clearly, emotions and feelings will be characterized by the concepts of liking or disliking. In each of these cases, the essence of liking or disliking is the feeling or emotion I have to a specific reality with which I am confronted. These feelings or emotions that are at the heart of liking or disliking can be very intense. They can either pull us toward another individual, situation, or thing or cause us to be repelled. Liking and disliking are appropriate concepts that can account for certain human emotional reactions. Similar to feelings, they are indicators of how we stand in relation to whatever is their object. They are also often fleeting, changeable, and experiences for which one can find oneself completely passive. Certainly one can dislike someone for good cause, but equally one can find oneself attracted to or repulsed by another without any identifiable cause at all. As we began this discussion, the question that is our focus has been the attempt to discover and give clarity to the essential nature of love and thus the specific role feelings may play or not play in the essence of love.

As with our other considerations, discovering the essence of love will require our grasping with a high degree of clarity what is essential to an act of love or to being in love. In other words, what is the element that characterizes love, without which love would not exist? In the process of achieving this objective, many wonderful attributes of love will be exposed that, while often desirable, are not necessary for love to be present. From our discussion above concerning feelings, it is critical that their role, as well as the role of our wills, be understood more specifically. One of the reasons for beginning this discussion with a focus on our feelings is because there is often a very tight connection experientially between how we feel and love. It is always important for us to acknowledge the experiential aspects of our lives. For this reason, beginning a discussion about the nature of love with the emotional experiences that very often accompany love is in no way misdirected. A lot can be discovered about love by starting with the affective aspects of it. Certainly this aspect of love often seems the most real to anyone who has ever been romantically in love. Human emotions are not the outcome of our wills. As such, the feelings, emotions, liking, and disliking are transient and can come and go, appear and reappear without reason. These are fundamental characteristics of human feelings and emotions, which can be influenced by numerous factors such as hormones, ill heath, and lack of sleep, stimulants, and countless other positive and negative factors that make them ill-suited as the sole criteria for prudent choices.

The first aspect of love that needs to be considered is whether feelings or emotions can be the essential characteristic of love. The answer to this question is clear when we relate feelings and emotions more precisely with the natures of liking and loving. When an individual says that he likes another person, what is it that is being stated? It is a statement of fondness. It is, at its most basic, a statement of one person's feeling about or for another. These feelings can take on a variety of dimensions depending upon their virulence and type: they can be feelings of affection, deep friendship, lust, hatred, indifference, or disgust, to name but a few. For this reason, it is not uncommon for individuals to like someone today, loathe him or her tomorrow, and be indifferent to him or her three years from now. That a feeling or fondness may last, lessen, or disappear is not a shocking phenomenon to most of us, for we have experienced this directly in our own lives or witnessed it between others. Sometimes these changes in one's feelings are based on specific causes and sometimes not. Understanding the concept of liking cannot be fully unraveled. However, understanding what makes it different from loving is essential. If liking expresses our ability to feel and to bond emotionally in our relationships, then loving, which certainly often entails those aspects, must entail something else, something additional and distinctive.

To discover the uniqueness of love more clearly, it may be helpful to state up front what needs to be established. While feelings and emotions happen to us and we are thus passive to them, love is an action of our individual wills. It is first the choice to be aware of the other and then the choice to be generous and courageous in doing the good that becomes apparent. As such, love is not necessarily transitory but has the capacity to be ongoing. This means that there are types of love that have the potential to be expressed in lifelong commitments. Specific acts of love can be expressed in shorter-term personal actions. In both cases, love requires acts of the individual will to be directed outward toward another. Offering a pregnant woman a seat on a crowded subway can be an act of love. It certainly does not entail a lifelong commitment, but it does include other facets that are always common to love. If this specific act is an act of love, it first requires that one be cognizant of a need. It then requires that one make a decision about how one should respond to this awareness.

Thus, in this simple illustration, the individual's noticing of the pregnant woman standing on a crowded subway is the first step in a potential act of love. It is for this reason that the human capacity to open up one's awareness is so critical. In this scenario, the gentleman may have had a long day and be tired out, annoyed at the crowded train and the heat, as well as preoccupied with trying to make yet another train to get home. The fact that he is able to place aside his own frustrations and be present to this young, pregnant woman is already a positive statement about the gentleman in question. So here we have a situation in which a gentleman is faced with a choice: to do nothing and just hide in his paper or to offer his seat to this young woman. It is now that the essential aspect of an act of love is made possible. The second and most important aspect of this scenario, if love is to be exhibited, is that the gentleman responds to what he perceives by choosing to do the good for the other. The first essential aspect of love that this scenario has presented is that love always requires the execution of the individual's free will.

The second essential element of love now exposed is that the choice must be for the good of the other. The choice to live our lives with attentiveness to ourselves and others is an essential predisposition of love. This openness to life around us and not just our own self-preoccupations is not a given in the often overcrowded world we live in. It is so easy to plug our ears with iPods or bury our faces in newspapers or completely focus our attention on our own feelings, thoughts, and concerns that make acts of love almost impossible. Nothing is wrong with an iPod, or the paper for that matter. The issue is to what degree we have as individuals or as a society shut ourselves away from the needs of our neighbors, our spouses, or our children. It takes energy, generosity, and a desire to engage and facilitate the possibility of love. It is through this first act of generosity, expressed in being attentive to another, that the foundation for love is made possible.

Love is, therefore, not linked essentially to the myriad of feelings that may accompany our experiences of it. The above scenario focused on love as the will to do the good one perceives, not for oneself but for the other. It did not necessarily require emotions as the pivotal drivers.

We would be seriously remiss if we were not to include in our discussion of love the kind of love associated with commitment. As most of us are aware, the notion of falling in love and then getting married is not universal in the world today, nor was it universal in centuries past. Hinduism, for example, still arranges marriages. For people in the West, this sounds barbaric, yet this practice was very common in the West for more centuries than not. What does the possibility of these arranged marriages reveal to us about love? In equal measure, what do the significant numbers of failed free marriages also reveal about love?

In the first scenario, two essential elements of love manifest themselves—choosing to be attentive to our surroundings, and then because of this, being open to discovering a need and choosing to respond to that need. Romantic, committed love is not essentially different in its components from individual acts of love. In a scenario where two individuals become emotionally involved and ultimately decide to marry, the success of that marriage will be based on the same elements described in the first scenario. The major difference is the role of emotions in the process of courtship and the decision to marry. As any couple who has been married for a good period of time will be the first to admit, emotions come and go, and the intensity of sex will vary in importance over time. With this said, assuming a normal pre-wedding experience and two genuine people authentically entering into this bond with the full intention of carrying it through, the subsequent success or lack thereof of the marriage will teeter on the same fulcrum as the act of love described above.

The first requirement of ongoing love is the healthy attentiveness of each party to both oneself and to the other. While this may sound trivial, it is probably one of the hardest aspects of committed love. It is so easy to think we know what the other thinks, feels, wants, and fears that partners often become completely disassociated without even knowing it. In the beginning of this text, we focused on the dimensions of humanity as always in-process and always a mystery to others and even to one's self. After being with someone for a number of years, it is easy to convince ourselves that we know the other. This can mean that we've pegged the other. This is the kiss of death for committed lovers. Essentially, it can mean we stop listening, seeing, and responding.

If love is to remain and be nourished, both partners must be absolutely committed to creating the space for the ongoing discovery of each other and their relationship. This commitment should optimally be a promised time that they create for each other and protect like one would a newborn. It will be the foundation for the love that must be expressed not only during this dedicated time but also between these intimate moments. How many marriages have begun on strong foundations but have allowed the complexities of children, social lives, and careers to destroy what were there and what was real? Committing time to one another that is regular (daily, if possible) is essential to protect the love two people have from the myriad of distractions, issues, misunderstandings, as well as the personal evolutions that each of us are undergoing without separating what was freely joined. As is apparent, love as an act of will is work. Love requires our commitment, energy, honesty, humility, as well as our ability to share our feelings, fears, and disappointments. In short, it means we must be willing to be attentive to our inner voice and the world around us. So much of what is important to relationships are the seemingly insignificant, small things that if missed, can begin creating a fissure between two people. For this reason, the first essential attribute of love is the gift of attentiveness to the other.

In the first book of Kings, this experience of how the call of love often happens is told in the touching story of Elijah, a prophet of God, who was completely fed up with the people of Israel. Elijah went into the wilderness and sat under a broom tree and asked that he might die rather than have to continue laboring to get God's chosen people to repent and turn back to their faithful God. An angel came to Elijah twice with food and told him to eat and to prepare for a great journey. Elijah was then told to travel to the Mountain of Horeb, which was holy to God. Elijah was obedient to the angel of the Most High and made the lengthy journey to Horeb. Upon arriving at Mount Horeb, God asked Elijah why he had ventured so far, and Elijah told God that he was at his wit's end. Israel once again had turned her back on God's commandments, and Elijah had done all he could as God's prophet to call his people back into covenant, even to the point where they were seeking to take his life. Elijah was fed up with Israel and wanted to die. God invited Elijah to go up further onto the mountain of Horeb where he and Elijah might share a more intimate exchange. Elijah did as he was commanded and went up to the mouth of a cave and waited to hear from God. First, a great wind came that rent the mountain and broke into pieces the rocks, but God was not in this fury. Second, a great earthquake came that shook the very ground, but God was not in the great strength of this earthquake. Thirdly, a ravaging fire engulfed the mountain in its rage, but God was not in this display of power and might, either. However, after the fire "a still small voice" wisped by, and Elijah hid his face (1 Kings 19:1–14).

Elijah's experience of the most profound reality of God is a paradigmatic truth about how the most important truths that we discover in our lives are most often conveyed. Often, the most important communications that we have or attempt to have with each other are in quiet whispers. If we are not careful, they can pass us by, leaving us completely oblivious. This myth expresses the very real human and spiritual truth that we are much attuned to the difficult, to the large or loud. The fact is that much of what is essential, wonderful, and central is not in these larger-than-life expressions. God knew Elijah's plight. God also knew what he was asking of Elijah: to love his people as he loved them. God's displays of wind, earthquake, and fire were not just for purposes of juxtaposition but to remind Elijah that he was God and he could end all of this in a nanosecond.

By juxtaposing these powerful acts, which did not contain God's voice, with a still, small voice that did, God was telling Elijah about the essential aspect of love. God made himself small, meek, gentle, and the unrelenting lover who would never cease to call back his bride. In short, God continued and continues to choose to love his people in their unfaithfulness. How could Elijah claim any more frustration, any greater right to anger than he who not only created Israel but who continually sent to her prophets to call her back to him? How could Elijah stand indignant before he who would never stop wooing his bride, no matter how far she wandered from him? God revealed that true love is a willed commitment to the other, often despite the other's fickle response. God made clear in this myth that, as his prophet, he would expect no less love from Elijah for his people than he, God, was willing to lovingly offer.

In Western society, where committed love and the procreation of our species are still expected to be highly emotionally charged, there can be an incredible burden on the two lovers to maintain this artificial emotional high. This is often maintained by the quick migration from couple to family and all the surrounding materialistic aspects associated with this. Happily, young men and women appear to be less trapped into the stereotype of the past. Sex and marriage are no longer intricately tied together as both science and morality have changed. This is not the panacea many thought it would be, since sex often replaces real intimacy. This model of sex released from the bonds of intimacy or commitment in many ways favors men who seem physiologically and psychologically to invest less in sexual encounters than most women. It is not unusual to hear of young women confused and torn by the fact that the implied intimacy they perceived was not there at all in the other party. In every relationship, there comes a point when the excitement of getting to know someone new and of sharing yourself with them begins to moderate in its intensity for one or both. It is at this juncture that the question of love becomes possible. Questions of what do relationships like this mean, where is it going, and the like begin to percolate above the emotional fray. For each, the issue becomes determining whether they are willing to love this person with these gifts and these flaws? For some, the next step is based on whether they believe they can change the other. A commitment based on either person's ability to change the other is doomed from the start. It is hard enough to change ourselves, let alone trying to modify another.

In those societies where marriages are still arranged, the extended family is a major support system for aiding the young couple toward mutual respect, knowing, and liking each other and ultimately love. The process and expectation of creating a family goes a long way in aiding this process. Successful committed relationships, regardless of whether they are arranged or free, must find a center based on shared values, principles, and the mutual appreciation that goes beyond youth, beauty, or material assets. The source of each individual's love for the other must continually deepen through a deepening interior appreciation of the essence of the other and the embracing of their entire person.

In the book *The Picture of Dorian Grey*, Oscar Wilde, the then-bohemian author, portrayed to his readers a horrifying story of a young man, Dorian, who was of incredible external beauty and the cost of this beauty, for it came without internal substance for this young man. The story hinges on the juxtaposition of the heightened external attractiveness of this youth with his equally heightened internal deformity, as expressed in his lack of human virtue, authenticity, generosity, empathy, and indeed his ability to truly love. Dorian revels in his own beauty and what it can bring to him. He fears nothing more than its natural loss, for he has set nothing greater aside as the fruit of his life. In the end, he makes a tragic deal with the devil for his soul. He is granted eternal youth, and in exchange, a painting of him both experiences the ravages of time and of his choices, which turn the beautiful Dorian as depicted in the painting into a grotesque monster. In time, Dorian comes to realize that pleasure without meaning—taking without the capacity to give—is itself a hell more unendurable than he ever imagined.

Dorian comes to experience the absolute emptiness of a life of self-indulgence, and he seeks his own end by confronting himself in the painting that once captured his beauty and now reflects back to him an inconceivable ugliness. The devil, having already known the tortures of eternity, knew the bargain originally made with Dorian held no risk. Dorian's soul was assured. The story of Dorian Grey is most apt for our time. It is a not-too-subtle reminder that the predisposition to love requires a certain emptiness, humility, incompleteness, openness, or receptivity to the other that creates a space from which we can be surprised, touched, indeed called out.

This first act of receptivity requires that each of us deliberately and consciously reassess our priorities, values, and principles and create a space for others by honest assessments of our lives and reconsidering how we truly determine our own individual value. Thus, this first act of the will that allows one to be able to love is itself an act of generosity, courage, and faith. It is the generous decision by an individual to attend to another and not, as is so easy, oneself. It requires courage in that the individual must believe that this reorientation is worth more than the possible pain that could accompany being rejected, ignored or belittled. It is an act of faith in that it would only be taken if the individual felt that by truly letting the other in, one might be able to affect something positive in the other as well as in oneself that would be worthy of the risk. At its core, the act of love is thus an act of hope. Hope in myself as the one who, through the act of self-giving, will be more than I am on my own. Hope in the other, in that the other as independent and beyond my ability to control and yet free to accept my offering of love or reject it will possibly open his or her heart to it. Thus this act of self-giving is an act of belief in the other at his deepest level, regardless of how my gift of love is ultimately received.

Both the New and Old Testaments abound with examples of everyday love and its centrality in expressing the values central to God's call to his people and his desire for us to be a community

(Leviticus 19:18). In the Old Testament, Mosaic Law was imbued with the call to Israel to love, first God and then the community of his people. This strong focus on love of neighbor is often expressed in the form of "thou shall not," but the underlying social implication is positive (Exodus 20:16–17, Deuteronomy 5:20, 23:19–20, Proverbs 25:18, and Psalm 15:3). God's love not only brings all things into being, but continues to sustain these things and reflects God's will to dispense his love on the good as well as the bad, on the righteous as well as the unrighteous. Jesus reflects on this supreme generosity when he notes that the sun shines on all people, not merely those who consider themselves righteous.

The New Testament is filled with stories told to make clear what the Teacher meant by love. The good Samaritan is the true neighbor who not only notices the man fallen by the roadside and wounded but then responds to what he sees by choosing to do the good for which the situation calls (Luke 10:25–37). Jesus' command that we not just forgive one another seven times, but seventy times seven times is another attempt at describing the limitless nature of love's generosity (Matthew 18:22). Forgiveness, as anyone who has had to forgive knows, is a very real outcome of our wills. Forgiveness can often require us to transcend our feelings and choose to let the trespasser back into our world. It can entail a great personal risk for the forgiver as he or she potentially opens him or herself up to being hurt once again. Forgiveness uniquely expresses key dimensions of love such as generosity, hope in the other, and the very real appreciation that we have also asked and required forgiveness in our lives. Forgiveness is a very real expression of love when it makes apparent the willed transcendence of the forgiver above the feelings of betrayal, anger, and alienation that can often accompany the experience of forgiving.

Love expressed in the commitment of two people to share their lives together in marriage is a very unique commitment informed by the same faith and hope required in individual acts of love. Few would argue that this specific type of love is a very real act of the will, because it involves an individual's commitment to the beloved, not just for a moment, but with the sincerest intention of "until death do us part." At the heart of this act are the foundational virtues of faith and hope. Faith is present in the couple as they embrace not merely their specific and immediate feelings and desires, but more importantly, in the open-ended promise to continue to choose to love the other into a future yet to be manifest. Their faith is not just in their own fidelity, but in the other's continued unfolding as an integrated and authentic self that is an essential aspect of the promise being made. Hope is essential as the basis for their ability to weather the uncertainties of their tomorrows, no matter what. This hope resounds in their mutual decision to bind themselves to each other with little to no ability to control how their lives together will unfold.

While the ideal of marriage should never be taken lightly, there are instances when the best of intentions can go awry. In cases where each individual's commitment to themselves, as well as to their betrothed, to continue their personal journeys of growth in authenticity is broken by one or the other, there may be a need to sever the relationship. While never ideal and always appreciative of the seriousness of this action, these decisions are not ours as Christians to judge. It is our call when such sad results take place to bring support, strength, and love as the healing balm of Christ.

As has been noted, love is not just pertinent to the realm of committed lifelong relationships, but also to the choices of self-giving that permeate the many uncountable moments of our existence and involve people with whom we have little or no ongoing relationships. Love is often shown when an individual chooses to hold their tongue, to spare a friend or colleague their wrath or "wit." Often real love can be discerned when one chooses to act for the apparent good of the other, even when the other rejects the gift of love or fails to see its significance. In these instances, it is all too human to become annoyed or angry. This response can be an indicator of just how truly our actions were done in generosity for the other or for ourselves. Love as a free gift is just as valid when it is rejected, spurned, or misused, because it is the quality of the free choice of the one who loves that makes it real, not the response of the person to whom it is offered.

There are as many examples of love that one might give as there are moments in the day and situations in which human beings are involved. The only elements required for love to be present are a human being with a will that is free, a spirit open to the world that surrounds them, and the generosity that enables the will to give what is required for the good of the other. Love is always an act of will and as such an act of self-giving. The feelings we have, which are a fundamental aspect of certain kinds of love, while not the essence of love, should not be trivialized, for they stand as indicators of what we experience. They should also not be confused with the love that may or may not emerge over time.

To make this point clear, it may be helpful to look at the concept of love as expressed in the language of the ancient Greeks. The Greeks had more than one word for love, which allowed them to express the many textures of love. These different aspects of love do not alter the essential nature of love as has been described above— rather they allow clarity around the fact that humans do experience love in varied ways. *Agape* is a complex word that grew to have many dimensions in the ancient period. *Agape* for the Greeks and early ancients always denoted a love that was self-sacrificing and volitional. *Agape* often described the love that existed between members of a family, divine love, or thoughtful love, i.e., a kind of divine love that had a sense of real generosity at its core. Certainly anyone who has been part of a large family can understand how this term could be used in both a familial context (by extension) and a divine context as well. It could also denote the love one has for one's vocation or calling, as this same kind of complete self-giving was often required in this context, as well. In the Christian era, this concept would be converted to the Latin term *caritas*. *Caritas*, from which we get the English word "charity," takes on the notion of the active and self-sacrificing love of one's neighbor, as well as the expressed love of God for humanity in the sacrifice of his son and its celebration in what was often referred to as the "Agape Meal," or the Eucharist.

Philia is the Greek word for the kind of love that would characterize friendships that transcend acquaintances. It is the appreciation by the Greeks that an acquaintance with whom there is a bond of fondness can become a friend but that this potential friendship is more than what existed before. What that something more entails, again, is the act of will of the two people to create a deeper bond. This bond or intimacy is a unique form of love, recognized and cherished by the Greeks as different from either *agape*, because it is specific to an individual, or *eros*, because it is not of a romantic or erotically oriented kind.

Eros is the Greek word for romantic or sexual love. Even here, the Greeks felt that the will should be involved. The Greek sexual norms were very different than twenty-first century middle-class conventions. Both the role of sexuality and its place within society were quite unique. For our purposes here, however, the point is that *eros* was a unique kind of love that included the giving of the whole person to another in a special way, but not merely as we think of as erotically. For the Greeks, the nature of an erotic relationship had multiple potential meanings and was not limited to the generative and familial context that has been the norm for much of the Judeo-Christian, Western tradition.

What often confuses liking and loving, feelings and choice, in our lived experiences are the processes associated with the development of human relationships. The process of attraction of one person to another is part of the natural progression of bringing people together. If this attraction is part of the romantic process, it can be very intense and operating on multiple levels. This neither makes the experience bad nor good. It merely is the first step in a natural process in which the possibility of love may be an outcome. Both the language surrounding this process and the process itself are open to much linguistic confusion, however. Within this process, terms such as "like" and "love" (especially in romantic relationships) are often used interchangeably. As has already been discussed, liking is based on feelings which are by their nature transitory and to which we are passive. Love, on the other hand, is an activity of the will and thus may continue forever. Love by its nature is also focused on the other, whereas feelings are internal dispositions of the self. These observations were reinforced even in the multiple Greek versions of the word for love, all of which required the will as central to their definitions.

Many of the aspects of love that have been highlighted have been ongoing themes, such as being attentive to life and others, having the courage and generosity to do the good when confronted with a situation, the ability to continually remind oneself of the eternal truth that both we and the other are mysteries to be cherished and that love requires continual effort on the part of both individuals. Love is also one of the clearest expressions of authentic relationships, for it necessitates the respect of the otherness of the other and the self-realization that no one will ever complete me. The will to love as has been described requires the full capacities of the human person. The will to love is also both the gift of God that enables each of us to become all that the architect of life intended for us, as well as our most perfect method of expressing the faculties that mirror the author of life.

In committed love, we are continuously called to choose to be and do the good that the other requires. It is an ongoing demand to accept myself and the other as unique persons deserving of ongoing respect, adoration, and attentiveness. It is the commitment to strive toward being the authentic self I am called to be and to always support the other in achieving the same. It is not a promise always to like each other. There will be times when couples or friends feel closer to each other and times when they feel more distant, for a variety of reasons. Loving is also a commitment to continue to engage with others and the world authentically, generously, and for the greater good. As has been stated above, this means embracing the other not in ways that attempt to annihilate the other's or my own individuality or otherness. It means accepting the loved one's otherness and calling forth their best self through our authentic presence.

Love is also a commitment to our own selves to continue to maintain the courage and fortitude of will required to authentically choose the self I can be. This personal commitment is expressed and lived out through the individual acts of love I express each day whether with friends or with complete strangers. As stated before, authenticity evokes authenticity. Choosing the good for the other is respecting his or her otherness and being willing to act to encourage his or her becoming the best self they can achieve. The concept of empathy expresses what is being described most clearly. Empathy is seeing the other from the perspective of the other and from that perspective, respecting his or her world as he or she sees and feels it. Empathy requires a true sympathy for the other. Rollo May, the famous psychoanalyst, once noted (I am paraphrasing) that the first act of love is in seeing the other. It is in the displacement of the self as the center of my egocentric worldview. This action is a choice, an action of profound courage, generosity, and dare one say, love. When it is not truly a gift of love, it will manifest itself as patronizing or belittling rather than respectful and nurturing.

Love and The New Testament

The New Testament concept of love as espoused by Jesus of Nazareth was clearly a love defined by the act of will. It was the will that moved the Good Samaritan to tend to the wounded stranger along the road. It was the will to be attuned to our world that was to be questioned at the end of our lives when we are asked about clothing the naked, feeding the poor, visiting the lonely, comforting the sick (Matthew 25). It is a love that was explicitly made active and associated with the will when Jesus stated, "Not everyone that saith unto me, Lord, Lord, shall enter into the kingdom of heaven; but he that doeth the will of my Father which is in Heaven" (Matthew 8:21). It is our will that is required in order to love our enemies and not just our friends, as demanded of us by Jesus himself (Matthew 5:17–48).

The will to love is a will that sees the other as a unique and wonderful expression of God's creative act, a mystery that is passionately searching for the self he or she was created to be and that can only be discovered in dialogue with the world of others. This means that the authentic self is always seeking to express its identity and at the same time discover this identity as it unfolds and continues to evolve. In discovering itself authentically, the self must give itself away. It must engage the people, situations, and events of life with true generosity. Literally, to "ex-ist" (Latin, *ex-sistere*) is to "stand out." This notion of the will to love, as a disposition of authentic self-giving, expressed in actions of generosity of the self, is critical to both a complete understanding of the proper disposition of self-discovery and the possibility of the salvation each of us is called to bring to each other and the world itself.

Generosity is being used in this context, not in the common sense of the sharing of the material assets one has, but as the acts of volition that include the sharing of one's person. This is done by an orientation of one's consciousness first, and then with it, one's will to choose to act as one is called to by the specifics of the needs of the other. These actions can be as small and as simple as a smile of recognition, the offering of a seat to someone who may need it, or a welcoming "hello" to someone who meets your eyes and has that tenuous look of fear so common in our world. Most of the time, these acts of generosity seem insignificant, but their impact is often larger than our immediate impressions. In some cases, we may be called upon to respond with larger acts of generosity, which may require us to dig deep into our internal resources, as they require our time, energy, and commitment. Often our modern society focuses on monetary actions as the method of being generous. This needs to be seriously assessed as a potential alternative to true self-engagement. Though for many this is not the case, it can be an easy trap.

The giving away of the self through continuous acts of authentic generosity is the mechanism of self-discovery and the possibility of bringing salvation more fully to the world and all men and women that share this world with us. As has been stated, the self and the world in which it resides are mutually constitutive. To the degree that the self engages the world and is continually called forth from its internal distortions through this engagement, it will discover its authentic identity. As the self engages this process, the world itself will be transformed. The more humans move toward authenticity and a proper orientation toward each other and the world of which they are composed, the more they will fundamentally change that world. This is at the very heart of the Christian vocation, which calls all men and women of good will to redeem this fallen world—fallen not due to original sin, but due to our choices to live lives of desperate isolation, self-preoccupation, and fear. Obviously, we do this as an expression of grace that has been freely poured out to one and all. It is by accepting this grace and enabling it to inform our very selves that we have the capacity to bring the kingdom that Jesus told us was already here.

The perfect act of the will to love, of generosity, depicted in the immolation of the Lamb of God, which is at the heart of Christian mythology, stands as the central paradigm of human self-sacrifice. "Greater love has no man than this that a man lay down his life for his friends" (John 15:13) can be interpreted not just as a call to the extreme of a bloody martyrdom but, even more essentially, as a call to the small but very real martyrdoms of self-denial and service associated with the small acts of kindness and thoughtfulness we are confronted with a thousand times each day. In an Old Testament myth (1 Kings 17:1–17), Elijah has been wandering during a great drought and comes upon a widow who is about to collect a little water to cook the last remaining dough she has with the last bit of oil for her and her son before they die. Elijah commands her to collect water for him and to cook some of the dough she has for him and then, after he has eaten, to cook what remains for herself and her son. This outrageous request by this stranger is followed by a promise that, if she follows this request, her pot of oil will never dry up and her jar of meal will never go empty. What a choice this mother was faced with: a certain meal for her son and herself or the promise from a stranger of meals forever if she sets her needs and her son's needs aside and provides him nourishment first. Her willingness to share what little she has, to choose to be generous, and to give the meager hospitality that she and her son have left and to accept the faith asked of her will end up delivering the outcome Elijah promises. The point of this myth is that the act of self-giving and self-sacrifice engenders life. This is a message much older and broader than Christianity.

Another place in which the essential linkage between humanity and its choices and the salvation that humanity has been called to participate in can be found in the central sacrament of the Mass. Going back to the Latin text, one can discover another critical dimension of the call of Jesus. In the Latin rite, the central verb that expressed the fundamental role of humanity was *"accipite,"* accept. Of the cup filled with wine, that night symbolizing the vessel of his blood, which he would offer for those men and all humanity—Jew, Greek, white, black—he stated *"Accipite et bibite,"* accept and drink. Of the bread that he took in his hands and broke, which symbolized that night his body, which he freely offered to be broken for those men and all humanity, he said again, *"Accipite et manducate,"* accept and eat. The unfortunate translation of *accipite* as "take" has expunged any notion of "will" in what was being asked of those participating in that most solemn of events. Jesus was not commanding. He was calling his apostles at the Last Supper to make an act of will by accepting both the cup and the bread, which he broke and offered to them. He is also calling each Christian at the Eucharist to make the same decision whether he or she has the fortitude to be broken and have his or her very lifeblood spilled in the process of giving his or her self away in service for the good of the other. The traditional "Amen" upon reception of the bread and/or wine was the receiver's acceptance of this commitment to take the path already trod; To follow the Master by choosing to accept and by loving as an act of engagement, not just in action, but also in the choice of meanings we create of our world and ourselves. In a very real sense, the Christian message was and is a vocation to redeem the world by redeeming each other and ourselves. The message of Jesus is not and has never been a faith focused on the next life, but on this one. Christ called us to redeem this world through acts of self-sacrifice, service, i.e. the will to love. It was his way and he declared, "I am the Way, the Truth the Life."

We would be missing a central symbol of the will to love within the Christian context if we did not spend at least some time reflecting on the cross as the premier symbol of Christianity. Whether one conceptualizes this image as the crucifix with the corpus attached or as the beam and crossbar is not important. It is these two pieces of wood, one piercing the earth and raised to the sky and the other stretched horizontally, yet affixed to the grounded post, which acts as the paradigmatic symbol of the Great Commandment.

This symbol reinforces much of what has been the focus of this work. Starting from an experiential perspective, the cross is embedded in the world. It is situated in the dust from which we all came and to which we all shall return. It is, like each of us, grounded in a specific time and place. Like all suffering, it is in the moment. At the same time, it points beyond this context to something more. It thrusts upward and out of the particulars of this moment, this event, and this context. It cries out that there is something greater than the moment, the individual, the sorrow and fear that I am feeling. There is hope. Hope not just in God, but also in each other and in ourselves as beings capable of bringing salvation to each other and our world. Thus, this vertical post stands not only for our rootedness in this world, but also the thrusting upward and outward of our transcendent natures, and as such, our desire to touch and be touched by the supreme Other, God. The horizontal beam symbolizes the communal context in which our very humanity and salvation are possible. For how can one love God who one cannot see and yet not love the neighbor whom one can see (Luke 10: 25–37)?

Thrust together as these two beams are in this horrible tool of destruction, we get the perfect symbol for the possibility of humanity's salvation, first our need to love God and, as a demonstration of this love, our neighbor. Suffering—as understood in the sense of the requirement to be acted upon and molded by life in the process of our ongoing self-creation and discovery—is also inherently acknowledged as the method of our individual and communal transformation in this powerful symbol. Any orientation of humanity's will that does not embrace these two dimensions, the horizontal and the vertical, in balanced focus will be a distortion.

This powerful Christian symbol often depicts Christ's arms pinned wide open upon the gibbet in a permanent gesture of inclusivity. This posture is no mere coincidence. Jesus' entire ministry was one of inclusion and of calling the purported outcasts to membership in the community. This inclusivity is a central tenet of the love we are seeking to understand. For love is not judgmental. It accepts the other as other. It seeks to serve the other by being the authentic self it is and to do the good it can do. Judgment is God's unique right. As Christians, we are called to be authentic witnesses of Christ: to serve the weak, feed the poor, listen to those who need to speak, care for the downtrodden, and strive for justice when it is denied to anyone. As Christians, we are called to remind each other of our radical freedom and its associated responsibilities and accountability. As Christians, we are to create the space for each person to discover the self- reflexive "I" that he or she is and its central role in the community's unfolding and salvation. No soul is unworthy; no person can be left behind.

Our language of exclusion can be subtle. Love the sinner, hate the sin; strict rules of who is "Christian," "Catholic," "Jewish," "Baptist," "Presbyterian" abound. "Come to me all ye who labor and I will give you rest" (Matthew 5:27–30). How much of our modern Christian rhetoric is based on fear, not hope; fear of the strange, the unknown, and the foreign? We must be a people of faith, a people of hope. The cross stands as a reminder to us that fear has no place in our hearts. The cross reminds us that suffering is but the means to salvation, not just as a means to a hoped-for hereafter via the resurrection but also for us here and now. Jesus asks his disciples when they are on storm tossed seas, "Why are you afraid…Ye of little faith?" (Matthew 8:26). Let this not be his question to us. All should take hope in these outstretched arms, for it is in that chosen posture that we see the foreshadowing of the mercy of our God.

Belief, Faith, and Prayer and Their Meaning in This World

The constructs we have been using have gone far in establishing a world based on God's desire to create a unique creature with the will to love him and the ability to be co-creators of both themselves and the world he initiated. In creating us with these capacities, God empowered humanity with great potential and even greater responsibilities. He enabled humanity with the ability to make choices, both individually and collectively, that would have implications far greater than either the individual or the societies that these individuals created could ever foresee. Combined with the non-moral causal processes or natural laws that are woven into the very fabric of all material-created things, we live in a world in which the apparent chaos of possibilities can bring about fantastic wonders, triumphs, saints, and alongside these the most incomprehensible atrocities, horrors, disasters, and evils. In the space required for God to create a being with a will to love, we have discovered the necessity for both good and evil.

Who is this God? We certainly have referred to him throughout, but can we ever really know him? Is he close at hand? Is he the God of the Israelites, the Christians, the Muslims, the Hindus, or any specific faith community?

It has already been stated, and probably needs to be reaffirmed, that God is ultimately a mystery. God is truly the "Other." As Thomas Aquinas was reputed to have stated at the end of his life, after all his many writings in theology (and I am paraphrasing), "I am left with silence." In the face of God's radical Otherness, however, a very real intimacy has been postulated, an intimacy based on the similarities between humanity as the potential image and God as the archetype. Through the myths that we have chosen to reflect upon, this intimacy was there from the very beginning when God decided to create man so that he might be capable of returning his love. This initial intent brought with it God's sharing of his own powers by giving both Adam and Eve their own wills, as well as imbuing this world with rational laws such as cause and effect, which provided the only context in which the human will could make sense. God's breath of life is humanity's first spark of being. Humanity's very nature as a being that can reflect on itself and its many states has been postulated as one of the facets of the Creator that was bestowed on humanity. Along with our ability to be conscious and reflective, God gave us a "will" which, though imperfect and constrained, is an image of the perfect and unconstrained will of the Creator. Our intimacy with God is not external to our natures, but is reflected in and through our natures. Our experience of our own capabilities, as well as our capacity to create both ourselves and our experiences, are but examples of the still, small whisper of their author who made us and loves us.

Can we know that there is a God? We most certainly can, but not in the sense that modern discussions about "knowing" would imply. When philosophers speak about knowing, or epistemology, they are describing the process whereby humans can grasp an idea and have a basis for claiming its veracity. These philosophers grasped long ago that some ideas have no corresponding physical reality to which one can point as a method of validating their "truths." In these cases, knowing is judged by the ability of the ideas set in some kind of relationship to coherently articulate meaning. An example of this more obscure kind of knowledge would be mathematical equations such as $2 + 2 = 4$. A famous English philosopher by the name of David Hume referred to these two methods of knowing as a fork, for if an idea cannot be empirically validated, I cannot point to it, then it must be a truth based on cogent rational definitions set in relationship to each other. The problem with the idea of God is that no one would be satisfied with a god as purely a concept in relationship to other concepts but without existence. If one claims that God exists, then there must be empirical evidence to support this belief, i.e., I should be able to point him out. Based on Judeo-Christian tradition, to see God would cause immediate death. Thus the empirical evidence required to satisfy science is highly unlikely. But the argument does not end there. For many believers, the existence of God is more real than many of our sensory experiences, and certainly for many, more relevant than most obscure mathematical equations.

So we have determined that the question of knowing God requires a different path, and thus our statements about God will always be somewhat unique. At best, our human categories will humanize God, and as a result, anything we say will be literally false. Metaphor, poetry, and myth may be our most appropriate ways, like David in the Old Testament, to dance around this mystery of God. Does God's ineffable nature mean that we can have no meaningful relationship with him? We have gone far to provide ample ground for a clear and resounding answer of "no." If a direct intellectual assault, based on our grasping human mental capacities to know, is not the basis for this relationship, what are the methods for being in relationship with God? The statement that we cannot intellectually contain the reality of God as one might of a mathematical equation or, any other normal perception we might have, does not necessitate a chasm that cannot be breached by either party. Nor does it mean that we cannot experience aspects of God if we are open during the course of our lives here on earth.

The first and most basic posture for understanding how we can have a relationship with God is a position based on belief. It is this non-epistemological orientation that is the key to grasping how humans can be both loved by and love a God without their ability to contain him mentally. Unfortunately, the meaning of belief has not always been clear even among those who claim to be believers. This lack of clarity centering on this pivotal concept has led to considerable miscomprehension about what we mean when we say we believe in God. This lack of clarity has been the source of much abuse by academics and has caused many young believers significant angst when confronted by their first few philosophy professors. It is important, therefore, to be clear about what this term means and what it does not mean.

Going forward, we will use the concepts of belief developed in *Faith and Belief* by W. C. Smith. Smith defines belief not within the constructs of intellection but as an orientation of the entire person to the object of belief such that their being is completely committed to its meanings, symbols, implications, and outcomes. Belief in God, therefore, is a fundamental commitment to God as the grounding principle that undergirds who I am, how I see myself in relationship to others and to the world in which I live. Thus belief pulls one away from epistemology and toward a lived orientation based on meaning. In less arcane language, since God is unknowable, defining belief as a category of intellection is meaningless at best. However, this in no way pretends to give credence to the narrow-minded, who claim that if something cannot be experienced with our senses, measured, and pinned down, it is empty of meaning. My claim that I love Sally may be true, but it is not something that can necessarily be discovered like a rock, nor is it merely an idea in relation to other ideas in my head. Most people would agree that if you knew me you would be able to see that I love Sally, but this would be based on inferences from my actions, words, and meanings. In this way, my knowing that I love Sally and the ability of other people to know that I love Sally is not so very different from how we know God. God is only different in that the believer's inability to know the divine is to acknowledge that the divine is not a fit object for our limited intellects and thus must be discovered through a different method.

The acceptance of a belief that infuses our life with meaning and is the basis of the individual's fundamental identity and meaning is the migration from intellect to existential awareness. This existential commitment enables the believer to experience aspects of God in her or his life. It is an acceptance that, while we may not be able to grasp the mystery of God with our minds, we can treasure the many characteristics of the divine that are so pervasive in the experiences of our lives. The completeness of God and our inability to intellectually contain him is not seen as a limitation in God, but rather a limitation in our faculties. Believing in God must entail that each individual's belief orientation infuses the meaning I give to myself and to others. When I say that I believe in God, I am saying that I am committed to the understanding of myself as an unfolding process in relationship to my world, which I am both creating and by which I am being revealed, and that I am being called to participate in the salvific process begun through God's creative act and continuing through each generation.

Thus belief is an act of will and not a particular or singular act of intellect. It is important to note that saying that God is not a proper object of our intellects is not claiming that belief in God is irrational or that our continued search for aspects of his reality are meaningless. It is rather just the proper understanding of our humble and incomplete capacity to grasp what is out of our potential scope. Not unlike many other facets of this work, our inability to grasp the mystery of God is, not surprisingly, equally true of our inability to grasp the mystery of ourselves or any other person. Yes, I admit I can point to you and thus verify your being, but the larger question of who you are is beyond both our capacities to contain.

Faith and belief are very different. When I say I have faith in something, I am stating that I have hope in the outcome. I am stating that the proper orientation of my being to a particular statement or set of propositions is one of hope. To have faith in the resurrection means to hope for it. I may also believe in the resurrection. The hopeful stance and the belief do not stand in opposition. In fact, belief and faith are coupled. One is a statement of my life orientation and commitment. The other is my humble realization that nothing is mine to grasp at, covet, or control. Hope is a posture of welcoming. It is the acceptance of the mysteries that surround us and the willingness to acknowledge that we stand in wonder and awe, waiting for life to reveal itself in its fullness as it will. Faith and its object, hope, are postures of trust, optimism, and a sense that there is meaning to life both in its largest sense and in the particulars. It is also the humble awareness that this meaning may always not be mine to grasp, see, or understand. It is for this reason that faith and its object, hope, are so important.

These concepts of belief, faith, and hope are also not just applicable to the divine, but also to each of us as unique individuals and how we stand in relationship to each other. As has been stated, each of us is a mystery, even to ourselves. The belief that the person I am is the outcome of my free choices of principles, meanings and symbols, as well as their implications and outcomes, is the primary step toward fulfilling my true potential. The next element in the process of self-actualization is faith, the faith required to have the vision and power to effect my personal transformation, for without faith I would lack the hope that this vision and power require. It is when this authentic self is offered to others in love that the possibility of personal salvation is given the fertile soil in which to bloom. How can we believe in God when it appears so many do not have this fundamental belief and faith in themselves or the person standing next to them?

Can I know God, therefore? Not in the epistemological sense used by academics. Can I have a real experience of the divine that can materially alter my life, my choices, and my ability to achieve the fullness of human existence? Absolutely, in the same way that I can discover myself, even though I can never truly grasp myself as an object. At best, I can only approach myself as a continual process of unfolding. My orientation toward God should not, in fact, be strange. It should be a very intimate pattern that I have discovered in reflecting on my own nature and on the nature of the human condition. For humans are always and everywhere subjects, and any attempt to objectify myself or another is not only to misunderstand the nature of who we are, but to repeat a pattern that has had dire consequences each time it has happened throughout human history. This fact is true, no matter whether one is speaking about the great wars of religion, politics, and greed or if one is speaking about brawls in local beer halls or on street corners or in schoolyards. In the process of reacquiring ourselves, our freedom, our subjectivity, and the possibility of experiencing the divine are realized. The bloodless exercise of intellectual religiosity and the vague notion of the self and God are replaced by the very real experience of my individuality and the divine as the very essence of the hum that permeates every part of our world and our experiences of life.

The next obvious question that one might ask is what role does God play in this model we have created? We have set up a world that God created with purpose and intention. He desired to create a being that could love him. One might be able to infer that he indeed has both concern and care for his creatures, as well. In fact, both the Old and New Testaments attest to this very fact, though each in its own way. The God of the Old Testament, while described as tempestuous, is certainly concerned and engaged with his creation. In fact, one could read the Old Testament as a very long love story, albeit a rocky one. The God of the Old Testament is certainly one of many different faces, but one thing is for certain: he is continually engaging his people. Understanding that the Old Testament is a particular community's history of its relationship with God over many centuries, it is instructive as a documented account of the evolutionary unfolding of their understanding of themselves and of their God and their relationship to their world. While their sense of who they were as a people certainly evolved and changed, so did their appreciation for their place in the broader world. Within the Old Testament, one can see many of the ideas reflected upon actually unfold. As Israel goes from being a small tribe to a nation, their sense of themselves and how that sense influences the way they treat other members of their community, as well as how they define non-members and how they are treated, changes. At the same time, so does their concept of Yahweh (God).

The God depicted in the Old Testament is, however, inconsistent with the concept of God and his relationship to humanity and the world being presented. In the Old Testament, God is continuously inserting himself into the natural order, either to fix things for the Israelites or to punish them. This is not a God who respects the world order of his own making. It is this concept of God that has caused philosophers and theologians to struggle with God's culpability in the world's evil. The Book of Job ponders this question when it depicts Job, an upright man, as being a victim of the devil's ill will. The devil prods God by postulating that Job's apparent devout nature is of limited value since he is well off and, therefore, it is easy for him to be a faithful Israelite. After some coaxing, God lets the devil have his way with Job to test the true mettle of Job's devotion. Job is thus visited with countless agonies to test his faith. In the end,

Job remains faithful to God, and the question of why evil happens to morally upright and God-fearing people remains unanswered.

The story of Job suggests that the problem that has plagued thoughtful believers is not new. If one asserts that God can insert himself here, then why did he not do something there? Once God is shown to insert himself into the events of human existence by altering the natural course of events, he then becomes responsible for the plague, the Holocaust, and millions of other atrocities, because in these instances, he did nothing. It is most emphatically the contention of this reflection that God does care. God does participate in the human experience but not in direct interventions into the natural order. These myths are telling of the experiences of communities that informed the meanings that the communities and the individuals discovered in their existences. The evidentiary details are missing the point of their telling. The fact that throughout Israel's history it saw the narrative of its people as directed by God's hand has little to do with whether Moses lifted his staff and parted the Red Sea or struck the rock in the desert and fresh water sprung forth. The belief of the Israelites in God's intimate caring involvement in their lives is expressed in many meaningful passages. Some of these passages use myth as an effective method of conveying truth and some may use facts.

In the New Testament, Jesus of Nazareth, an itinerant rabbi, announces to the world into which he arrives that he is the Son of Man. He preaches a new twist on the teachings of the prophets. He announces a new era and calls the community of believers to a radical reorientation of their thinking. He does not destroy the past but reframes it. He revitalizes the Spirit of God within this community by reaching into the essence of their meanings and values and exposes the accretions that clouded, and in some cases refocused them over time. But in the person of Jesus, there is a radically new relationship being offered between God and his people that is different from any that had ever been offered before. One important facet of this new relationship—the fact that St. Paul was to make the cornerstone of his life's work—was the true breadth of Jesus's invitation. No longer was it to be assumed that only the children of Abraham were to be invited to the banquet. St. Paul, known as the Apostle to the Gentiles, not only ensured that anyone could be welcomed as a follower of Jesus but also that he could be welcomed without becoming a ritualistic Jewish person first. What is important to note is that God is no longer just making himself manifest to the children of Abraham, but also to his numerous other children as well. Is it impossible for us to conceive that God is also making himself known through such messengers as Mahatma Buddha, Mohammad, Zoroaster, Confucius, and many other prophets? If the answer to this question is yes, then the necessity of discernment in discovering those who truly can aid us on our unique journey becomes one of the most important skills to develop.

The development of an anthropological view of humanity that has attempted not only to clarify what humanity is essentially but also what humanity's fundamental uniqueness is relative to any other created being has been a central goal of this work. This fundamental power in humanity is its will to determine its own meaning and the meaning of the world in which it participates. As has been previously stated, all actions are subsequent to this fundamental action of the will to choose the symbols, images, and meanings that I use to construct myself as a pre-reflexive "I" and the world that I thus perceive. It is by hearkening back to this facet of ourselves that we can discover the point where the mystery of God and humanity's intimate connection with God came together in the full creation of the human person. Jesus' coming into the world could be considered as an intrusive insertion of God's will upon humanity. In many ways, this depends on how one sees Jesus and how one reconciles the belief that he is the unique Son of God with his very critical humanity. While the Church has wrangled over how to articulate this mystery almost from the beginning, it is ultimately a mystery. We can, as communities of believers, articulate our statements of belief and attempt via our language and our limited understanding of reality to express the proper boundaries of our belief systems, but we should never forget we have not obliterated the mystery which remains at the core. Jesus' incarnation does not have to entail the invasive act of God in human history.

So how do we come into the presence of God, if not through reason? And even more importantly, how does God dwell among us as a caring and loving Creator without rending the space required for our free response of love for him? Prayer is the mechanism for reflecting on a specific and powerful interaction point between God and humanity. A common criticism of prayer from those outside the community of faith has always been that it is a superstitious act of the supplicant asking God to change lives. This criticism is based on the view that the prayer is nothing more than a primitive form of incantation with expectations of miraculous outcomes ranging from physical cures, winning the lottery, getting a job, curing world hunger, selling a home, to almost anything one can imagine. Certainly one cannot argue that at various times each of us may pray earnestly for some kind of external intervention by God. This aspect of prayer is a dimension of prayer that is both real and all too human, but to assume that it is the most important thing going on or the only thing going on is to miss the essence of this critical activity.

There are many aspects of prayer that can be considered. One is the psychological aspect of prayer in which the supplicant, as the person in need, is experiencing both the powerlessness of her position and her fear, loss, desire, and hope. Prayer provides a unique context in which a person of faith can articulate to herself and God not only how she is experiencing what she is experiencing, but also the many textures of this experience. For example, in the case of a recent death of a spouse, the bereaved widow will often truly express her loss to herself for the first time within the context of prayer. It is within this context of a dialogue with God that so many of our deepest feelings, hopes, desires, and fears can be expressed not just to him but to ourselves. Once expressed, they become exposed and at a purely human level, unlocked and thus available for further working through. From this perspective, therefore, prayer is a very meaningful context in which a person of faith can release feeling, emotions, and thoughts not just to have them linger but to enable them to be made more real and more clearly understood. To claim that the meaning of prayer stops here would be to seriously limit its value and to miss its real point entirely, for prayer is not merely a psychological tool through which we discover our feelings. Prayer is much more.

C.S. Lewis, having been asked why he prayed, answered, "Because I have to." This aspect of prayer is truly its essence. It is a view of prayer as the symbolic act of placing oneself in the presence of the "Other" in order to both present oneself and to be reordered in and by the experience. In the act of praying, I present myself and I sometimes present petitions, not just to another human or even to myself, but more importantly, to one greater than I, the one I hold to be central to life. Unlike any other activity that I do, when I pray (authentically pray, as opposed to a flippant statement such as "Please, God, let him hit this ball"), I place myself before the Other as the supreme transcendent, the Holy and Sacred. No matter whether I am in a place of worship or in a car, on a bus, or in my bed, I am placing myself in a unique place that is made sacred through my meanings. In the act of praying, no matter how ill-defined, I am transforming my place into a space that is sacred.

By creating this sacred space, the person makes available to himself or herself an entire set of meanings and symbols that attach themselves to the individual's awareness of the transcendent, no matter how tentative or how ill-defined. In the act of praying, whether using ordinary language or traditional formulas, one is opening up one's self-reflexive "I" to the possibility of seeing and integrating a deeper and more profound set of meanings about who one is and the nature of one's world. It is this possibility that the moment of prayer offers that is the essence of prayer. It is this potential expansion of the self and the opportunity of the self to discover new possibilities of meaning that can challenge potentially inauthentic dimensions of the self and foster greater openness, awareness, generosity, and service. In prayer, the self and its temporality are placed in juxtaposition to the "Other" and its eternality. The "Other" as the truly transcendent offers alternative ways of seeing or being that do not alter the external world but potentially alter the subject praying.

The space of prayer for the believer is not just one of a fundamentally reoriented sense of time, but also a space imbued with sacredness. For a Christian, this space is alluded to in the first and most sacred of prayers passed on by Jesus himself, the Our Father. The phrase, "thy Kingdom come, thy will be done, on earth as it is in heaven," is not just the call for the ultimate arrival of the end time. It is a call for a transformation within each of our souls. It is a call to increased receptivity to a new way of being, of a new way of existing in this world, which will truly bring about a new world and a new people. Within this context of teaching his disciples to pray, Jesus is not only sharing a form for communicating with the Father, but reveals the message and meaning of such divine-human dialogue itself. This context of meaning we call prayer requires that the self, as supplicant, expose its own willed meanings, not just merely of the prayer, but also of its very being within this sacred milieu of eternity. As one prays, one exposes the willed meanings that underlie who one is—one's values, prejudices, fears, hopes, anger, as well as one's longings to be more than one is. All of these aspects of the self are exposed within the safe pleas offered in humility, existential vulnerability, and mystery.

Prayer exposes to each of us the possibilities of the real power that each of us has to choose the selves that we can be and the ability to bring love and life to those whose lives we touch. Our prayers may not be able to change external realities of life, but they can be the mechanisms for our own continued transformations, which will have incalculable effects on our world. It is true that Jesus said that anything we asked of the Father in his name would be given. This statement should be understood as more profound than our ability to ask for material things. It must be understood within the realization that God does not experience time and events as we do, for as we have discussed, these phenomena of space and time are our methods of experience. Asking God for something and understanding the answer received must be within the larger context of the good that God always will choose in spite of how at this moment and in this circumstance it may appear. Jesus also clearly stated,

> Ask, and it will be given you; seek, and you will find; knock, and it will be opened to you. For every one who asks receives, and he who seeks finds, and to him who knocks it will be opened. Or what man of you, if his son asks him for bread, will give him a stone? Or if he asks for a fish, will give him a serpent? If you then, who are evil, know how to give good gifts to your children, how much more will your Father who is in heaven give good things to those who ask him! So whatever you wish that men would do to you, do so to them; for this is the law and the prophets.
>
> Matthew 7:7–12 (RSV)

The Buddhist tradition also builds on this concept of prayer as the context in which the soul can come into contact with the true, the eternal. Through the discipline of creating a space for a new kind of listening, the Buddhist seeks to hear from a different perspective. In most of our lives we hear from the perspective of our needs, wants, fears, and desires. This is egocentric listening. The Buddhist, through meditation, seeks to open up a different perspective (what is often referred to as the third eye) not of the ego but of existence as it is. This ancient tradition has much in common with Christian prayer.

Mature Christian prayer requires an openness and emptiness that only God can fill. Prayer is not just done in need or want, but in a desire to meet and discover the "Other" and in doing so, to come to greater understanding of self and place. The monastic custom of "centering prayer" is the Christian corollary to the Buddhist tradition of meditation. Unlike other forms of prayer, centering prayer requires the person to become still, and through consistent and purposeful attention, to let go and just to listen. This ancient form of prayer is not easy, especially for men and women of the twenty-first century who are used to constant activity and internal and external noise. But it is both effective and achievable. It is the practice of making oneself available to God, not through the mind and ideas, but at a much deeper level. It requires the one meditating to allow one's thoughts and wanderings of imagination to flow past like a leaf carried by a river. Over time and with practice, the internal noise will diminish and soon one will be able to sit in the presence of the mystery of the "Other," as well as the mystery of oneself.

It is important to understand that prayer is always a dialogue by its very nature. Prayer as the act of opening oneself up to the "Other," no matter how ill-defined in the belief system of the supplicant, is still in its very structure dialogical. The individual that prays is placing his pleas, hopes, pain, joys, and awe before the eternal mystery of the "Other." In this act of self-exposure, the individual is at one moment opening up herself and her ways of experiencing her world to the "Other" with whom she is engaging in dialogue. This is at its core an act of self-exposure. The very meanings that are the self and the world the self perceives are opened for possible reassessment in juxtaposition to the meaning and transcendence of the "Other." My experiences, with all their aching reality, are placed before the transcendence of the "Other" and seek to find their right place and perspective. The eternal "Other" stands juxtaposed to my lived temporality as a being in time. The eternality of the "Other" calls out my temporal experiences to find their meaning within the larger context of both my own time and eternity.

In this respect, prayer can be a mechanism for conversion of the self from inauthenticity to authenticity. Prayer is truly the place in which we meet God as the "Other." This meeting is never a context in which the "Other" will take away our otherness through intrusion, but as the one who calls forth our authentic selves to full life. In this way, prayer is both a source of personal actualization and salvation. It is thus also the source of renewal for salvation, not just for the individual praying, but also for the community and the world. The ability to pray hearkens back to our discussion concerning our ability to listen, to hear, and to dwell. The stillness that prayer demands is a precondition to our hearing, not just on a human level, but also on a spiritual level. Understanding both the human and the spiritual dimensions of dwelling or of developing the discipline to create a space in which we can be present to ourselves and to God is essential to the unfolding of the entire person. What can be more important than creating the context in which each of us can discover the truth of ourselves? If it seems frightening when one first tries, this may be an indicator of just how far we are from ourselves.

The Incarnation— Immanence and Transcendence

The desire not merely to expose the fullness of the meaning of being human, but having done this, to revivify our Christian faith as something not foreign to our human natures, but understood as intrinsic to their completion has been a motivating factor of this work. In order to achieve this objective, it is essential that the person of Jesus be a core part of this discussion. Everything preceding has had its place in setting up a thoughtful gaze upon our faith and its relationship to whom we are and who we have been called to be.

Within this journey there has been little desire to dwell on the historical Jesus. While academics within this field have added much to our understanding of the man Jesus, and his times, this path can be perilously devoid of meaning and, in many respects, an inappropriate attempt to rend the Christ of faith from the man Jesus, as experienced by the early Christian community. As was noted at the beginning of this journey, the methods of the early church in sharing what they perceived as the essence of their experience of Jesus is very foreign to our modern methods. In juxtaposition to the historical approach, we are dwelling on the texts as provided to us and eliciting from them insights that can demonstrate Jesus as one of us, and then to reflect on his more complete nature as the Christ of God. This method continues to elucidate the miraculous within the human, as told through the numerous rich myths that comprise the New Testament. In all humility, much of the wonder and magnitude of Jesus, the man and Christ, the fullness of his meaning, is neither within this author's capacities to adequately explore, nor is it in our scope.

A meditation on Jesus and his meaning has a natural starting point in the Gospel of St. Luke and the story of the nativity. One could certainly have chosen to begin the reflection with St. Matthew's focus on the coming of the messiah within the milieu of his place within Jewish history as the long-awaited messiah of the Old Testament. Saint Matthew references numerous Old Testament texts, which Jesus's life fulfills. St. Matthew's gospel spends considerable effort tying these events recorded about Jesus's life up within the larger theme of Israel's fundamental belief in a longed-for anointed one who would be the ultimate priest, prophet and king of Israel. The highly spiritualized path of St. John's gospel, which sought to articulate Jesus' life using the symbols and language influenced by Greek culture and philosophy, could have also been an interesting point of departure. This Hellenistic influence provided both a language and many philosophical constructs, which would be fundamental to the early Christian Church's development of a Christology which would aid the early Church in articulating the mystery of the intertwining of the human and divine dimensions of Jesus. Since we will be focusing on St. Luke's gospel as the jumping off point of this rumination, there will be certain differences that will result from this choice. For example, St. John's gospel develops a true Christology and could be said to be more representative of a descending theology. By this is meant that St. John attempts to see Jesus from the perspective of the fullness of his identity as the second person of the Trinity. Thus the Gospel of St. John begins very differently than the version of St. Luke that really is more representative of an ascending theology, *i.e.*, from the Church's experience up. This truth can easily be demonstrated by quoting the beautiful opening lines of St. John and comparing them to St. Luke. St. John's gospel begins:

> In the beginning was the Word, and the Word was with God, and the Word was God. He was in the beginning with God; all things were made through him, and without Him was not anything made that was made. In him was life, and the life was the light of men. The light shines in the darkness and the darkness has not overcome it
>
> John 1:1–6, RSV

In this opening of St. John's gospel one can immediately see that this is a descending articulation of the Church's understanding of Jesus' life, as it begins with the relation between God as the author, or metaphorically the one who speaks creation into being, and Jesus as the utterance, i.e., the Word, uttered by God in the act of creating. This intimate unity of oneness is the launching point of St. John's entire gospel. St. John also introduces the notion of light as an ongoing theme associated with Jesus' mission and the mission of all those who follow him. For our mission is to both be the light of the world and to spread this light to rid the world of shadow and darkness. For St. John, Jesus is both co-creator with the Father and the emanation of the Godhead's perfect source of life and being. All of these images would have been powerful to the Hellenistic Jewish community and the Hellenistic world.

In opposition, as we have noted, St. Luke begins his gospel:

> In as much as many have undertaken to compile a narrative of the things which have been accomplished among us, just as they were delivered to us by those who from the beginning

were eyewitnesses and ministers of the word, it seemed good to me also, having followed all things closely for some time past, to write an orderly account for you, most excellent Theophilus, that you may know the truth concerning things of which you been informed

Luke 1:1–5, RSV

As is apparent from the beginning, St. Luke is not going to present a Christology, as does St. John. He wants to relay to his reader Theophilus ("lover of God") the pertinent meanings and wonder that he and his companions have shared and continue to share with each other. Thus, as an ascending view this approach is much more amenable to the questions we have been opining about, which are focused on our humanity and its relationship to the Creator and thus to Christ.

Far greater and more spiritual men and women have reflected on this mystery of the incarnation for millennia. The path taken here will borrow from many of these masters and yet will still seek to be its own personal meditation. It is not our intention to be dogmatic or even an academic articulation, rather a meditation on key aspects of the life of Jesus with which we are presented. In fact, our meditation will focus on a very small portion of the entire picture. Our objective is to expose, by means of dwelling on aspects of this unique manifestation of the immanence and the transcendence of Jesus, the magnitude of his person and its direct implications to us who call ourselves his followers at both a human and a spiritual level. At its core this dwelling asks each of us to honestly assess who Jesus is for us, as individuals and as communities of believers. In so doing, we are opening ourselves to a kind of scrutiny that is based on who we are, what drives us, what nourishes us, what beckons us, and most of all, what grounds the self that we are and that we are willing to become.

Using St. Luke's account of the man Jesus as written to Theophilus and a piece from St. Matthew allows us to begin our journey with one of the most beautiful myths of the New Testament, the incarnation. The incarnation myth presented in the Gospel of St. Luke has many foreshadowings and antecedents that make choosing a point of departure somewhat arbitrary. Our dwelling on the incarnation myth could legitimately start deep within the Old Testament and God's promises made to his beleaguered people through numerous prophets for a messiah, king, and priest. It could also start with the birth of John, who will later be called the baptizer. John is often considered the last of the Old Testament prophets. John's conception by Elizabeth, the wife of Zechariah, already casts the shadow of mystery and wonder onto this person, John, as Elizabeth was a woman long beyond her child-bearing years. The events that unfold in the lives of both John and his cousin Mary, the girl who will become the mother of Jesus, are tied together at the very beginning of St. Luke's gospel. John's life will also be significantly intertwined with the yet-to-be-born child of Mary.

Mary is the daughter of Joachim and Anna, and has lived her life in the obscure village of Nazareth, an occupied part of the Roman Empire. The incarnation myth, described in the Gospel of St. Luke, states that on one ordinary day, Mary is met by a messenger of God, the angel Gabriel, who announces that the Almighty has chosen her to conceive a son: "and (he) shall be called the Son of the Highest" (Luke 1:32). Mary, who is believed to have been about fourteen, was understandably startled. Regardless of Gabriel's assurances that she should not be afraid, this encounter itself must have been terrifying. Gabriel continues with his purpose, which is to present to her a proposition. If the circumstances were not already somewhat surreal, he then provides the details from the author of the proposal, none other than God: God's desire to bring a child into this world with her cooperation, for the benefit of Israel. Initially, she reverts to the practical issues that surround this picture by informing Gabriel of a most personal fact, that her being with child is highly unlikely as she has not yet had relations with any man. The angel Gabriel, knowing that she has not completely grasped his proposal, makes it clear that God would be the father of this child. Gabriel then reiterates his message as a request of her to accept God's offer to bear his son. Gabriel then awaits Mary's answer.

Imagine what must be going through the mind of this young girl. *Who is this with whom I am speaking? He has told me that he is a messenger of the Most High. What can it mean to be Yahweh's son? Why am I, an ordinary Jewish girl, being asked to participate in such an remarkable request?* All Mary knows is that, if she accepts, this son, her son, "will be great, and will be called the Son of the Most High; and the Lord God will give to him the throne of his father David and he will reign over the house of Jacob forever; and of his kingdom there will be no end" (Luke 1 31–34). The images invoked by Gabriel are rich in meaning for any Jewish person of that day. David represented a time of Israel's zenith. This child is promised to bring back this kingdom, no longer as a temporary moment in history, but forever. These words, rich in meaning, are being spoken to a girl who lives in a time of foreign occupation with a corrupt King of Israel who is a mere puppet of Roman might. Whatever must have been whirling in her thoughts, Mary finds a place deep within her where she can focus and dwell on the request being placed before her. This internal place must have been the core of her faith and strength, for from this position Mary replies with her humble affirmation of belief and faith when she utters, "Behold the handmaid of the Lord; be it unto me according to thy word" (Luke 1:38).

This moment of Mary's *fiat* (literally, "let it be so") is, unbeknownst to her, the beginning of a new era. Upon this maiden's "yes," the world would be set on a new trajectory. On this simple yet unfathomable act of submission, God is given permission to merge the ineffable and uncontainable with the specific and limited. It is impossible for us to know what Mary was thinking as she humbly accepted God's offer. What is clear is that all the particulars associated with this *fiat* were incidental to her complete faith and complete submission.

Throughout history, many have questioned the orthodox Christian veneration of Mary. What many have failed to realize is that it is the moment of her *fiat* that defines both this maiden and her deserving adoration. For what Christians see in this young maiden is the archetypal human response to God that few of us, and even many of the great saints, have been unable to achieve. For each of us is called in a similar manner, as this young girl, to embrace what we are being called to be and how we are being asked to play our role in salvation history. Many of us have experienced moments when we have not had the capacity of faith, humility, or hope that enables such a response. This myth and Christian tradition are quite clear. Mary's *fiat*, "let it be so," was absolutely required for the unfolding of the subsequent events. This *fiat*, the maiden's complete act of her will to love, could not be contained within her and poured forth when she later greeted her cousin Elizabeth, already pregnant with John, in one of the most beautiful prayers ever given voice, the *Magnificat*, or "the Magnification."

> My soul magnifies the Lord,
> And my spirit rejoices in God my Savior.
> For He has regarded the low estate of His handmaiden,
> For behold, henceforth all generations shall call me blessed.
> For He who is mighty has done great things for me,
>   and holy is His name.
> And His mercy is on those who fear Him
>   from generation to generation.
> He has shown strength with His arm:
> He has scattered the proud in the imagination of their hearts.
> He has put down the mighty from their thrones,
>   and exalted those of low degree.
> He has filled the hungry with good things;
>   and the rich He has sent empty away.
> He has helped His servant Israel, in remembrance of His mercy;
>   As He spoke to our fathers, to Abraham
>   and to His posterity forever
>   Luke 1:46–56, RSV

Thus begins the first act of the God of creation in the Christian New Testament. The Almighty bends down and requests that a girl of fourteen cooperate in salvation history. The all-powerful Father begs his creature's aid. Is there any more powerful image of the centrality of the human will in God's salvific plan? Does this beautiful myth not confirm God's choice not to interject his will intrusively into humanity's context? This *fiat* places Mary on the road of misunderstanding, social disapproval, and uncertainty. This perfect will to love with all its characteristics—generosity, other-centricity, the desire to do the good as it is made clear, and the postures of hope and faith—will continue to be required of her as the mystery of her child and her life continue to unfold.

As the angel promises, soon Mary is with child. Now the reality of human life meets the transcendence of human love. The cost of discipleship (which almost two millennia later would be the title of a book by another holy man, Dietrich Bonheoffer), would now expose itself in the human reactions of those who would discover her pregnancy and who would choose alternative explanations which were far less noble, burdened as they were with prejudice, judgment, and their consequent actions. As the myth claims, Mary was betrothed to a man named Joseph. As was the custom, she and Joseph had not taken up residence together and thus had not shared marital rites. When Joseph discovers she is pregnant, he is shaken and shamed. By law, Joseph had the right to expose her. This would have meant that she could have been stoned. Joseph did not desire to do this, but was unsure whether he wanted to make her his wife. The myth states that an angel visits him in a dream and tells him that Mary is with child by the Spirit of God and that he should not be afraid to take her as his wife (Matthew 1:19).

Again it is important to note that the angel did not command or threaten or even shame Joseph. He explained to Joseph that he need not fear and made a statement that must have seemed as strange to Joseph as it would to any one of us, that the baby in his intended's womb was the fruit of the Spirit of God. The nativity narrative does not linger on Joseph's reaction to this dream. There is no description of how this dream was received. Certainly, its meaning and veracity must have taken him some time to grasp. Whatever the process or whatever internal agony Joseph went through, the authors of this myth wanted us to focus on the fact that Joseph, too, was now to make his own real choice. Joseph's choice would be a choice very similar to that of Mary, a choice based on belief and fundamentally expressive of his faith and knowledge of Mary. Joseph made the decision to take Mary as his wife and to raise the child as his own. Again, the human will is required as the necessary prerequisite for the divine plan to unfold. Joseph's will to love, his generosity of spirit and trust again enabled God's salvific plan to proceed.

It was required by Jewish law that the first-born male child be brought to the temple and a sacrifice be made to God. As she and Joseph proceeded with Jesus, they were intercepted by a holy man, Simeon, who took the child in his arms and confronted her with words that would provide a glimpse of who this child was and her intimate connection with his mission.

> Lord now lettest thou thy servant depart in peace, according to thy word; for mine eyes have seen the salvation which thou hast prepared in the presence of all peoples, a light for the revelation to the Gentiles, and for the glory of thy people Israel… Behold, this child is set for the fall and rising of many in Israel, and for a sign that is spoken against and a sword shall pierce your own soul also (referring to Mary), that the thoughts out of many hearts may be revealed
> Luke 2:20–36

Mary had already experienced many real costs of her *fiat*, but here was a holy man making clear to her that this small child would cause much turmoil, would suffer himself and she with him. What is essential to pause and dwell upon, is that time has not been opened up so either she or Joseph could see what all this foreboding language would mean. The process of life that is filled with uncertainties, fears, and concerns was not altered for her or her child. She, her husband, Joseph, and her child, Jesus, would discover who they were and what their role was to be, as every other man women and child since the dawn of creation. Faith, hope and the all too real aspects of human existence as being comprised of a journey in which each step is characterized by uncertainty was to be their experience, as it is ours.

Outside of the question of a Christian's beliefs about the factual elements of the texts discussed above, it is important to grasp the centrality of the human will in the fulfillment of the divine intention. The question of the way in which Mary conceived is bound up in belief and mystery. What is not open for question is the centrality of her will. She stands for Christians as the exemplar of all those who strive to align their wills with the divine. Her *fiat* stands as an act of awe-inspiring courage, hope, humility, trust, authenticity, generosity, strength, and love. Her *fiat* is itself the purest of prayers. This simplest of maidens, Mary, has inspired and humbled the greatest and the lowliest of men and women for over two thousand years. She stands as both our exemplar and as our fellow journeyer. Her nature is purely human, as is her husband's. As a mother, she achieves yet another dimension of approachability that few archetypes can evoke in modern Western culture. This fact is made clear in the rich art that surrounds her image throughout various cultures and through the centuries. Mary is most always depicted as the bearer of Jesus, as the lowly maiden humbled in the very act of being chosen, and as unconditionally obedient. In a world in which marriages are preceded by legal documents defining the conditions of separation or divorce, Mary stands as the bride unconditionally participative in the love being offered and responding with her entire being.

At the very beginning, we posited a view of humanity that positioned the creature and creator, humanity and God, as potential and actualized reality. Humanity was defined as the only creature with the potential to be the image of God, not by any act of God's external will, but through humanity's exercise of its own will, the will to love. Not every Christian theologian has held this specific view of the intimate relationship between humanity and God. Saint Augustine claimed vehemently that between the creature and the creator there was a chasm that could never be filled. While this view has certain merits in understanding humanity's ability to know and immerse itself in hedonism, egoism, selfishness, and cruelty, it is an incomplete view. It certainly makes perfect sense if one understands Augustine's own life and journey to God. In many ways it is a much more existential perspective, for it expresses the reality that as a species, very few of us have come close to the image we were created to achieve.

Much later in history, another great saint would opine on Augustine and his chasm. St. Thomas Aquinas was a theologian of the scholastic period. His brilliance is still a matter of considerable amazement to Christians and non-Christians alike. Aquinas knew well of our complex natures and he acknowledged equally our capacity for inconceivable evil and our limitless ability to love. Through his ongoing study of the human spirit, Aquinas came to a very different conclusion concerning humanity. First, Aquinas believed that one did not exalt God by denigrating his paradigmatic creature, humanity. Aquinas believed that there was no inherent chasm between humanity and God. He firmly held that actualized humanity, in fact, is divine. It is in this sublime truth that the possibility of the incarnation, as yet another example of the act of the human will and the possibility of humanity's salvation, becomes plausible, not as a foreign intrusion of the external hand of God, but as the truly awe-inspiring fulfillment of his creative will. For Aquinas, there is no doubt that Jesus is a unique manifestation of humanity and creator incarnated. However, this uniqueness is not a wall that separates Jesus and humanity. Rather, it is a challenge to humans to discover their calls and to align their wills to the essence of their beings. In Aquinas's concept of salvation, we are each called to be the method of salvation for each other. The secret of this alignment is in our willed capacity to love as we have already been loved.

Jesus of Nazareth, whose nativity story displays the nexus of the human will and the divine intent, is at the heart of the ongoing journey of God's creation as it seeks to come to its fulfillment. This man Jesus, who was flesh and blood, became the Christ. This transformation was one of tremendous significance. It is not a mere shift in moniker, but an essential shift in his followers' understanding of the person Jesus within the larger context of their faith. This evolutionary process experienced as part of the journey of human experience and unfolding is intimately tied to humanity's coming to a complete understanding of the nature of Jesus, but is not claiming that Jesus' nature is altered by our evolutionary processes. The transformation of the individual flesh-and-blood man Jesus, who existed in time and space, into the Christ, who is and was and always will be, is a fundamental shift in meaning, which the disciples and the early Church were to grasp and place at the center of their faith.

The early Christian community experienced a fundamental change in how they chose to see this man Jesus. As the Christ, Jesus is making God present in a new and unique way, but not in a way that must, by its definition, disregard God's respect for the human will. In fact, Jesus the Christ is the full and complete actualization of that will, now oriented to its one true object, love. It is in this sense that, when we hear people say that God is love, we can understand the truth and immensity of this equation. The mystery of the incarnation, which is the manner in which God made himself present in Jesus, remains forever a mystery. Christ is a unique manifestation of God. The incarnation is consistent with the constructs of either God's initial desire to create humanity as a being with the will to love or our need to respect the inherent mystery that must remain central to this most sacred of events.

The fundamental anthropology presented herein posits a view of humanity that is not fundamentally different from its source, God.

From this point of view, there is no inherent conflict in apprehending Jesus as fully human and fully divine. The advent of Jesus on this earth and the belief of his followers that he was the Christ of God can thus be approached as not some magical transformation from humanity to creator, but as the willed choice of a fully actualized human being responding to the full potentiality of his being created from the beginning by God. This perfect response of love, this perfect alignment of will, effected the fulfillment of the unique union of the archetype, God, and the image, Jesus, in time. If we start from the presupposition that Jesus is completely human, the process of his unique unfolding and actualization become both important and instructive. Unfortunately, we do not have significant accounts of his youth and adolescence. In fact, until his entry into his public ministry, there is silence.

What is critical to keep in mind is that, like any person, Jesus had to mature and slowly come to an understanding of himself as a person, just as each of us has. To conceive of Jesus as living his life fully conscious of his Creator would be to make an assertion of his full humanity absurd. The process of becoming or self-actualization could not be in any way different than the processes and challenges that we have focused on and that we experience as central to human development. In fact, an essential prerequisite to understanding both the gift of Jesus and the cost of his will to love is to be very careful of removing the man Jesus from the human process. Jesus discovers himself in choosing to align his will to that of his Father.

Over the centuries, artists and writers have introduced methods of seeing Jesus that have, unfortunately, so stylized his humanity that many of us have become forgetful of his flesh and blood reality. Losing sight of Jesus as a real human being is both dangerous and all too easy. The minute Jesus becomes something different from us, we can become disconnected from his complete self-sacrifice and its very real call to each of us. Only when we de-mythologize him and again allow his humanity to come forward can we participate fully in both his message and its price. It is so easy to forget that it was a man who bled, cried, and pleaded in Gethsemane that he might be spared the oncoming ignominy and agony. This was fully expressed in Jesus' prayer, "Father, if thou be willing, remove this cup from me: nevertheless not my will, but thine, be done" (Luke 22:42). This prayer perfectly demonstrates his choice to embrace his future not as an act of passivity, but as an act of love—an act of his will. Luke goes on, "And being in agony he prayed more earnestly: and his sweat was as it were great drops of blood falling down to the ground" (Luke 22:44). It was also a man who accepted the cross as his personal choice as the fulfillment of his Father's request.

Without our truly appreciating that this was a true flesh and blood person—who had no sense of the completed picture, who, like us, stood as an individual of belief and faith, who had to face the mystery of himself, others, and God—we will be unable to appreciate both the miracle and sacrifice that was Jesus. Saying that Jesus was not completely cognizant of the mysteries which humanity must come to accept is in no way to diminish his person. It does cause us to pause and take into account that the gospels were written after his life was over. Consistent with the position taken from the start, these gospels were not written as *New York Times* articles, with all the facts and details that we are so used to. This reality requires us to stand back from the gospels and their rich truths and appreciate that they wanted to relay to us the essential aspects of this man's life, death, and meaning. The vehicles they used to pass on their life-changing experiences so that others could grasp the unfathomable meaning of this man can give the impression that for Jesus there was no mystery, faith, or belief, for he knew all. I believe this is a serious misunderstanding of Jesus and of the tools used to convey truth with the facts which were to these writers secondary to the message.

Jesus did not go to the cross complete with the sense of inevitable personal victory. Jesus went to his fate as a man. He felt the blows of abandonment, physical pain, misunderstanding, fear, and shame. None of these statements belittle the Christian belief in Jesus as the

Christ. In fact, it is our core belief that our true acceptance of his humanity can only elevate our numbed apprehension of him and the miracle of the incarnation by removing the veil of mystery that has separated Jesus from us. This separation has allowed us to escape our personal responsibility by focusing on his Creator—and thus on making him so very other than we are—and thus the reality that his life choices and their costs were less costly than they were. It allows us to convince ourselves that he was so very unique that his call to us to be "Christs" to each other is quaint, but quite impossible. In some senses, we have allowed ourselves to be dulled into a stupor. We have placed Jesus on our altars, on great mosaics, canvases, in carved plaster and stone carvings, but has his courage in doing his Father's will been lost in this process? By embracing his Creator, did we create our own escape clause? Has the distance between the haloed Christ and the man Jesus become so great that we have forgotten the reality of the personal costs to him and thus, to reuse a phrase coined by Dietrich Bonheoffer, the real "cost of discipleship" for each of us?

It is not coincidental that this same cost and this same acceptance of God's will as the unknown journey of faith were the patterns previously established by both his parents. Both Mary, in her *fiat*, and Joseph, in his decision to embrace the mystery of this child's birth and take him and his mother to himself, were no less real acts of the will to love expressed in their openness to God's call to to become what they were in potency. The early church fathers fought long and hard over the question of Jesus's identity. They struggled about the question of how to characterize him, because they understood the implications of overstating one side of his nature at the expense of the other. Is it also possible that they indeed foresaw the subtlety of the human soul and its cleverness in avoiding the radical nature of Jesus' call to us, his disciples? If they had overstated his reality as Creator over his reality as human, it certainly would have called into question the degree of imitation of his life to which his followers were being summoned. The Council of Chalcedon, which finally decided on this question by claiming that Jesus was fully human and fully divine, clearly desired to avoid Jesus' extrication from the human condition and the weakening of the radical implications of his message to his followers' lives. This fact causes one to ponder the famous quip of G. K. Chesterton, that it is not that Christianity has failed, but that it has never been tried. When one stops assuming that Jesus had all the answers, and that faith and belief were unnecessary, it is then that the fullness of who he was and is becomes painfully clear in its relevance to who we are and are called to be. It is also from this perspective that what it means to be Christian begins to take shape and the centrality of the will to love makes sense.

Like Jesus, who walked to his death fully cognizant of its reality, we too each begin this journey to our deaths the day we are born. For most of us, however, this realization only begins to sink in as we mature. As young men and women, many of us are able to keep this reality as far from our consciousnesses as possible through focusing on the infinite aspects of our lives and our capacities to manage life with its many demands. At some juncture, however, the reality that each of us is not eternal does begin to slip through. This realization is essential to our proper progression as mature human beings. For some of us, the catalyst may be the death of a parent, spouse or child. For others, it may be the slowing down of our own progression in strength. Whatever the immediate cause, this coming to terms with our transience is not an easy realization. As anyone over 50 begins to experience, there is a letting go that life begins to place in front of one. This letting go comprises such things as the increasing loss of loved ones and the slow realization that we have neither the energy nor strength of faculties which we may remember so fondly as part of our youth. It also can entail the reassessment of our expectations of what we should have achieved in this life, as well as a complete reorientation of our values and the life we have left to live. This slow stripping away of externals, whether of power, a sense of infinite time, or the deterioration of physical youth, strength, and beauty, can truly be a real aspect of our personal Gethsemanes.

A critical facet of our personal self-actualization is how we face this process. Just as with our abilities to accept the otherness of people played a core role in our growth in authenticity, so as our beings follow their natural journey of growth, strength, diminishment, and death, we are asked to embrace this process with the same faith, hope, and generosity. Through this embracing of the critical dimensions of our own subjective processes described above, power, money, beauty, and strength will be placed within their proper context. This process offers to each of us the opportunity for what is real to become more apparent and the exposing of many of our own false gods for what they are. This stripping of the accidental elements of who we are can enable the essential core of our beings that we have built throughout our lives as a result of our choices and the principles and values that have informed them to become visible. In this respect, the process of aging is a wonderful process of the human journey in which the false will be peeled back like an old skin with the opportunity of revealing a new self now exposed in truth with the potential for changes and adjustments and for an increase in our own lived authenticity.

The incarnation stands as the ultimate exemplar of the unity of creator and humanity. It also stands as the inescapable grounding of the message of Jesus of Nazareth to each Christian to take up his cross and follow him as no mere metaphor. Jesus' will to love was a radical answer to what he heard his Father asking of him. His message, as recorded in the gospels, the letters of St. Paul and the Acts of the Apostles, outline a specific worldview, a new view of the relationship between God and humanity and its tie to our relationships to each other and a new way of assessing what is important in life. Jesus' absolute humanity offers no hiding place for us. There was no special gift or palliative for him, there is no secret he had that is unavailable to us. Our call, like his, is to accept the radical freedom that we are. Jesus' identity as the Christ, the anointed, the savior, is, in a derivative sense, ours as well. We have been called to participate in his vocation. We must carry on, indeed bring to completion, what he has started. It has been over two thousand years, and we have only to look at our world to assess the quality of our labors. It is only by accepting our uncompromised freedom, potential, and accountability that humanity's capacities can be realized and the world that is us can be transformed. It is not our governments, religious institutions, schools, and businesses that must change and that are called to transformation; it is our selves that must change, and these other things will follow. This focus on institutions is often a focus on symptoms as a deflection so we do not have to face the real causes, which are our selves. The only hope we have in changing these complex institutions is in fundamentally accepting the burden of responsibility that is our own personal transformation.

Within the Buddhist tradition, it has always been stressed that the apparently insignificant act of a single individual can change the world. This appreciation of humanity as not just a billion instances of specific human beings, but the highly interconnected and interdependent oneness that is as real as our perceived individuations appears also within the later developed theology of St. Paul. In Christian terms, Paul contends that the Christian community, as the real ongoing manifestation of the body of Christ, is this unity and oneness. It encapsulates his call as well as the continued aligned will between Christ and God for the redemption of all of creation through the Spirit that was sent to provide humanity its ongoing grace. To say that humanity's salvation, as well as all creation's redemption, is our essential mission is not an overstatement. Regardless of race, ethnicity, even creed, we are all part of an ongoing and all-encompassing task to bring creation to its goal, its fulfillment through the proper aligning of our wills with that of our Creator. Within this context, we are given our ability to understand and assess who we are, who we will be, and how our ways of being bring meaning, light, and life into our world.

One of the great temptations that all of us face as part of life is the temptation to despair. Despair can be defined as our choice to focus on the darkness, the shadows that we all discover in ourselves, in our lives and our world. It is often driven by fear. This fear can be the realization of our inability to control, which is a truth we must all embrace. We can choose to look at life and focus on the shadows and darkness that elicit the fear that is always there, or we can choose to focus on the giftedness of our lives. This choice of where to place one's attention can truly determine our capacity to live. Our daily waking and the realization that we have another day to be and to choose how to be, is the first and most basic gift. To wake and be healthy is another gift that we seldom bring to mind except when we are ill. To realize our many blessings in light of the millions who may have so much less is a choice to focus on the light and life. It also evokes in us a desire to give of our bounty to others, whether it is in the choice of disposition we take or in the choice to be more cognizant of our world and the people that we shall meet and a determination to bring more joy to that world as a result of how we live this day.

As a unity, humans are often oblivious of the very intimate interconnectedness that expresses this unity. How I am can and does often influence others who interact with me. As a general rule, do people walk away from me feeling taller or smaller than when we met? Does my way of living bring out the hope and joy in others, or do I revel in the aspects of life that darken my world and that of those around me? Spiritually, despair is a very powerful tool for evil. Like its positive counterparts, it can paint the meanings we choose to place at the center of our lives. This despair is as much a choice as its opposite, gratitude. By no means is anyone belittling the real suffering and pain that is an inherent part of life. This reflection is claiming as loudly as possible that the meaning we choose fully cognizant of life's hardness is not a necessary outcome. True joy, true peace does not obliterate the pain of life, but are the chosen refusals to make them the complete and total meaning of our lives and life in general.

Sin and Forgiveness in the Will to Love

The concept of "sin" is unique and worthy of consideration within the context of the framework of the will to love. As with so many of the realities that have been part of this journey, it will be critical as a first step to demythologize sin to see if and how it relates to the understanding of what it means to be human and, most especially, *authentically* human. The classical definition of sin, through St. Paul and the Greek tradition, has the literal meaning of "a missing of the mark" (Greek, *hamartia*; see Romans 3:23), as in the metaphor of a bull's eye and the deviation of an arrow from its rightful focus, its center. Sin is thus, in its most direct meaning, an action or set of actions that deviate from whom we were created to be and how at a particular moment we are being called to respond.

Holding aside the question of what "the mark" is, it is important to delve more deeply into the active nature of sin and its relationship to the anthropology postulated in this work. Sin, as activity, is certainly consistent with the concept of humans as beings whose fundamental capacity lies in their agency, *i.e.*, their capacity to will. This more enhanced notion of will can potentially broaden and expand the relevance of the concept of sin to be discussed by adjoining it to all its textures. The concept of activity is too coarse. If left as is, it could give one the impression that sins could be defined simply as a laundry list of actions such as stealing, lying, murder, adultery. If this were the case, then why bring it up? Certainly, this is the common understanding that most of us hold and we would be merely repeating the obvious with little value if it were taken as adequate.

If, however, the notion of activity is not accepted at such a coarse level, if the concepts elucidated within this reflection on the role of the will within humanity, especially as regards its self-creation, the creation of the world in which it abides, and the nature of true freedom, then there may be more here than the traditional image of an accounting approach of our actions that so many of us were brought up with. The concept of will, which has been central to our definition of the human person, as well as inherent in humanity's expression of its myriad of capacities, has consistently entailed a much richer view of its corresponding responsibilities and potential points of accountability. From these perspectives, the notion of human agency as will and its potential influence on the nature of sin do have a critical part to play in a development of the concept of the will to love.

It is the realization that humans, unlike other creatures, can deviate from their instinctual path because of their will that makes a concept such as sin meaningful. From the perspective of the will to love, the concept of sin as "missing the mark" adjoins itself fittingly with the principle of human agency, expressed in the co-creative aspects of the self and thus our ability to move both away from and toward its desired end. The concept previously introduced—that each person is created by God as a potential that can only be actualized through each person's individual acts of will—centers human agency as the heart of our will and at the very apex of the concept of sin.

Sin, as a "missing of the mark" within this context, must be considered as the will's lack of proper orientation in bringing forth the self to its fullness. As a result of the mutually constitutive dialectic of the self and the other, this lack of proper orientation of the will, which can diminish the self, must also, by definition, diminish the other. The concepts of authenticity and inauthenticity, developed to describe the two alternative extremes of interacting between the self and the other, can now find expression within the context of a meaning of sin as a "missing of the mark."

As unique children of God, we have been created with an internal trajectory to become what we were made to be at the beginning of all creation, when the author of our creation had as a blueprint who we could be. This call at the core of our existence always remains a beckoning. Sin, as defined as the deviation from this potential, thus describes the results of our choices. St. Augustine believed quite differently. Augustine believed that within the very core of humanity was the tendency toward sin, the result of the disobedience of Eve and Adam in the garden. This predisposition, resulting from humanity's first act of disobedience, was dubbed concupiscence, which means a natural tendency toward sin. For Augustine, baptism was the only cure that could remedy the sickness that he saw at the heart of our capacity to will. Aquinas did not accept St. Augustine's interpretation of the myth of Adam and Eve and thus did not consider our expulsion from paradise as a fracturing of our perfect natures. This does not mean that St. Augustine did not grasp a very real truth about our natures. For who among us cannot relate to the experience of temptation that seems to draw us away from what we know is right? Even Jesus acknowledged this reality when he stated, "The spirit is willing, but the flesh is weak" (Matthew 26.41). This existential reality does not, however, necessarily demand that we understand the human will as deformed. It demands an understanding of the truth that the will is free and that often what is good or right is difficult and extracts a cost that individuals are not always willing to pay.

Unfortunately, humans have used the concept of sin for their particular purposes, and have, over millennia, warped and twisted its meaning and thus its richness. The concept of sin has been sullied by how it has often been particularized in time and place. Thankfully, neither these misuses nor their unfortunate outcomes have tarnished what can be a very helpful reality for those trying to understand and live the call of the will to love. Historically, the issues concerning sin have been in the particulars. At a conceptual level, the idea of "missing the mark" seems understandable enough. Even the notion of understanding that sin must concern itself with acts of the individual will or the collective will (communities, by extension) in opposition to some standard seems rational. Things have gotten very complicated when that standard has been posited as God's will.

This is where humanity has often found itself in a very difficult spot. For who is the rightful determiner of God's will or, using our definition of sin, who determines the locus of the "mark" and thus our missing of it? For many faith traditions, such as Judaism, traditional Christianity, and Islam, the community in some combination with God's sacred text has been a determiner of what is or is not sin. In some traditions, more emphasis has been placed on the sacred text and revealed commandments and/or laws, such as the Decalogue and the laws of Leviticus for the Jewish community. In most cases, however, while a sacred revealed text can be the basis for some defined sins, it is seldom the sole source. In many ways "The Book," which for Christians is the Bible, contains numerous principles of right living but does not address the infinite subtleties of our lives and the choices we are confronted with. Humanity also requires its own community to be capable of reflecting on itself and its times. In addition, each human being has been provided a conscience at the very core of our beings. Based on this the question of where can we look for proper guidance on how to live our lives requires more than a sacred text. The question is what more this might be and how can we ensure that whatever it is, it is a proper guide.

Within the Christian tradition, there are two major perspectives on this question: the prereformation perspective and the reformed perspective. Interestingly enough, both of these views would agree that both the Bible and the church are the rightful determinants of defining sin (as specific kinds of actions), not however, in determining whether a person has actually committed a sin. This distinction is subtle but important, and will require clarification. Where the Reformers and the prereformation faiths' communities diverged was in the meaning that was to evolve around what each meant by "church." In the prereformation traditions, the church was understood as composed of two very different dimensions, the people of God and the church as the "Bride of Christ," the "Mystical Body of Christ," the perfect and incorruptible jewel that transcends all humanity's bungling and imperfection. This aspect of the church is considered as expressed in and through the Apostolic Succession, the direct descendents of the apostles; in the West, the bishops in union with the pope in particular, and in the East, the bishops in union with the patriarchs. This view is often based on such passages as, "Verily I say unto you, whatsoever ye shall bind on earth shall be bound in heaven: and whatsoever ye shall loose on earth shall be loosed in heaven" (Matthew 18:18).

Thus, for the Catholic faiths, the bishops and the pope in the West and their counterparts in the East have the ability to define sin. In the Reformed traditions, the church was redefined as the community of believers in much more immediate union with the Bible, thus removing the hierarchical, civil (monarchical) structure that took hold within the clerical structures of the pre-reformation churches and, in some cases, expunging any kind of clerical structure at all (as in the Society of Friends). Sin was thus defined within the context of the Book and the sacredness of the community itself.

It is necessary to briefly outline these historical differences in order to set them aside and postulate another way of viewing sin. While the same word will be used, because of its incredibly rich meaning and existential power, its association with the above religious history can only distract us. Previously, the notion of "the mark" was put aside so that the idea of agency could be deconstructed into the finer elements of "will" and its proper objects.

Now it should be possible to readdress the question of what exactly the "mark" is that is either being hit or missed. Unfortunately, this metaphor is not as exact as the metaphor of the bull's eye. At the individual level, the "mark" is the self that we must discover and have the courage and generosity to become. Notice the lack of definitiveness in this statement. It is not an attempt to be ambiguous, rather a specific reassertion of the absolute first principle that each person is a process of unfolding and a mystery even to himself or herself. Life is the ongoing process of self-disclosure, which does not, however, mean that there is not a self to discover and a "mark" to hit. The previous discussions concerning the calling forth of the self by the world (people, situations and things) and the proper posture of authentic responses and their characteristics create the arena for honing in on the "mark." This is the key characteristic of the "mark" for humanity. It is not a clear spot, staked out and stationary. It is dynamic and ephemeral. It is very real, but not graspable. It is as vital, as we are vital. It is the goal of our lives and the object of our becoming to continually search for and hit this mark. By extension, therefore, it is not just the mystery of myself, but the very mystery of the other and the mystery of our community, society, and world that we are acknowledging, yet again, in this ongoing groping for the "mark" in each and every act of our will. For in each moment there is a mark that we must strive to hit in acts of authentic openness, awareness, and responsiveness to what is before us.

It is this simplicity, and the seeming insignificance of what it means to hit the mark, that makes it even more difficult. If hitting the mark involved huge acts of magnanimity and generosity, it would in some ways be easier for us to accept. To claim, however, that hitting the mark is first and foremost to be attentive not just to the other but also to ourselves, and then to choose the good that is apparent, does not articulate the full complexity entailed in these acts of personal agency. It is for this reason that the great faiths have all prescribed the consistent practice of listening, of being still and dwelling. It is also for this reason that, in order to be a Christian, one must also make consistent time to immerse oneself in the Bible and the lives of the saints and holy men and women of any faith tradition. To discover the mark and hit it, one must be aware of three things: the other, the self, and the moment in which these converge. The further one lives from the actual moment, the now, the more daunting the task of hitting the mark, which is always and everywhere in the now and not ever in the past or in the possible future. Thus, the mark, which is the image that we formed to actualize, and the Creator are only to be found in the now.

While the specifics of the mark are not always detailed, we have been quite careful to identify some of the common attributes of the mark that are universally apparent. We know that the proper orientation of the individual will, as well as the collective will, must be one of authenticity. This authentic orientation always accepts the subjectivity of the self that I am and the subjectivity of the others that they are and requires that the inherent mystery of both be acknowledged and respected. Very practically, this necessitates avoiding the real temptation of categorizing, labeling, or objectifying either myself or the other. It is having the courage to allow myself and the other to be surprised by who we can be from moment to moment. It entails the radical courage to be able to allow myself and the other to transcend our previous experiences, limitations, and failures and be willing not to lock down our self-identities or those of others by preconceived expectations and fears that are molded from a hardened, rigid, and non-evolving sense of the self. It is being willing to have the courage to be and to let another be as she is.

In this acceptance, each person is acknowledging once again the inherent mystery of himself and of the other and the always-prevalent capacity of the human will to transform who we are into who we may be. Every time we objectify another by writing him off because of some act of unkindness, we are closing the book on him and his ability to be other than he is. This may sound terribly theoretical, but it is critical to state when discussing the all-too-human habit of categorizing people based on their past actions. This penchant can be devastating to the authentic unfolding of a person's individual self. Anyone who has lived past the age of childhood has most certainly had numerous experiences in his or her life in which he or she made mistakes or participated in regrettable things and learned from these and moved beyond them only to find that the people with whom he or she interacted refuse to let go of their preconceived notions of this past persona. This inability to allow the other to grow and to evolve can be an indicator of a lack of generosity that manifests an orientation of the self that is hardened and may be indicative of a vengeful and mean nature. Allowing each person to manifest his unique internal blossoming without the prejudice of past experiences painting old faces on new persons is an act of generosity; it is also an act of self-recognition and humility, for it is an acknowledgement that each of us has fallen and must ask no less from each other.

Prejudices based on race, creed, social status, sexual orientation, or whatever else humans can concoct to objectify the other, are all just twists on this same theme. All sin is in some way related to the eternal dance of the self and the other. To the degree that our orientations toward ourselves, toward others, and toward the other become inauthentic, there is sin. The degree of sin can only be determined by how extreme our choices of meaning and the actions that flow from them deviate from our call to the will to love. This willed posture to shut another out is the very denial of the spirit that dwells deep within them, as well as our call to be authentic and never deny anyone their subjectivity, vitality, and capacity to be as they might be. It is within this context that Jesus' admonition, "Judge not, and you will not be judged; condemn not, and you will not be condemned…Why do you see the speck that is in your brother's eye, but do not notice the log that is in your own eye?" (Luke 6:37–39,

41–42 RSV), not only reveals the fullness of its meaning, but also its consistency with the inclusivity of his life.

Hitting the mark is also having the courage to be able to stand up to those who cannot tolerate such authentic expressions of the self and to demand the appropriate respect for each person's individual will to love as the basic expression of being. For sin has more than its individual dimensions. As beings in and of the world, we must respond to any injustice. It makes no more sense to perceive oneself as on the mark while blindly walking past injustice or participating passively in acts of exclusion or hatred than it would if we actively participated in these acts.

Any discussion of sin as a falling short of the mark must entail an equally balanced understanding of the concept of forgiveness. The idea of forgiveness is a complex one for, if not considered carefully, it can have many misleading connotations. At first blush, forgiveness may seem to set up a dichotomy between the one who forgives and the one who is forgiven. Outside of a proper context, this orientation could be construed as a power dynamic between the one seeking and the one conferring forgiveness. Jesus attempted to make clear the leveling aspect of forgiveness in opposition to the concept of power within the prayer he taught his disciples. It is no mere coincidence that the "Our Father" or "Lord's Prayer," has in it the phrase, "Forgive us our trespasses as we forgive those who trespass against us" (Luke 11:4). Jesus clearly meant to have his followers continuously keep in mind that forgiveness is something we offer not in self-righteousness, but in humility as ones who have themselves been forgiven. In another teaching Jesus again states, "forgive and you will be forgiven; give and it will be given to you; good measure, pressed down, shaken together, running over will be put into your lap. For the measure you give will be the measure you get back" (Luke 6:37–38).

To place forgiveness within a power framework is to distort its purpose and its meaning. The challenge is to discover the correct context in which this existentially profound reality can be unpacked without distortion. It is within the will to love that this contextual meaning of forgiveness is revealed. Forgiveness is an act of an individual's will. This fact should not surprise anyone who has ever had to forgive someone in his life. Like every other question, the issue with forgiveness is what in particular is the "will" up to in the specifics of the act of forgiveness?

In order to obtain some clarity about this complex notion of forgiveness and the role of the will within it, it may be helpful to reflect on this concept in Judeo-Christian history. In ancient Israel, the Jewish people would often beg God's forgiveness through fasting and acts of mortification, such as covering themselves with ashes (a tradition also common among the Hindus and other religions). Forgiveness was and is a key part of the Jewish faith and culture. The communal heart of Judaism not only encouraged the acceptance of sincere contrition between members of the community, but they also formalized it in their holiest of days, Yom Kippur (the Day of Atonement), when each member of the community was required to ask forgiveness of those he had offended and not previously approached. In addition, the high priest, as the representative of the entire community, would take two goats, one to sacrifice in the temple and the other (the Azazel goat) onto which the high priest would symbolically place the sins of the entire community. That goat would then be released out into the desert to symbolically carry away the sins of Israel (Leviticus 16:22). Here it is apparent that Israel had a deep appreciation for two very critical aspects of forgiveness: its individual and communal dimensions. Later, Christianity would build on this Jewish tradition by carrying forward these two dimensions.

With the advent of Christianity, forgiveness was not to lose its centrality. Jesus was very concerned about forgiveness and spoke about it often. He told his disciples that they should forgive seventy times seven times (Matthew 18: 21–22). In another place Jesus says, "And when you stand praying, if you hold anything against anyone, forgive him, so that your Father in heaven may forgive you your sins. (Mark 11:25). A final example that should not be overlooked is demonstrated in one of the last utterances attributed to Jesus while he was hanging on the cross. This utterance beseeched his Father to overlook the unforgivable betrayal of his son when he cried: "Father, forgive them; for they know not what they do" (Luke 23:34).

The early church maintained this rigor concerning forgiveness with the development of confessing. (This concept of confessing in the early church had little in common with the much later development of the Roman Catholic sacrament of confession.) In the early church, confessing was an act of the community of faithful. The church, being small and usually centered in compact communities, would gather and publicly proclaim their faults to each other and receive the corresponding communal absolution. This new twist of publicly proclaiming one's faults and then receiving forgiveness within that same public context takes the social and personal dimensions of the Jewish tradition and adds yet another texture to it. In this way, confessing was not organized to undergird a power base for those with the ability to forgive. On the contrary, all of the community stood together in fellowship and humility, fully realizing their need for each other to continue their ongoing struggle to live the life of the Master. To have been forgiven by each other is the great leveler that ensures that the distorted potential position of power in being able to forgive becomes the greater folly. This tradition of communal proclamation and forgiveness was carried forward in the Benedictine tradition of the "Chapter of faults," during which the monks would not only accuse themselves in front of the entire community, but also one another. Benedict's vow of stability, required of each monk, ensured that the spirit of charity would infuse this process by the very glue of living together with the same community till one's death (*The Rule of St. Benedict*, prologue).

Reflecting on these developments adds numerous dimensions to the concept of forgiveness within the overall milieu of the will to love. First, as has been illustrated, sin is the will's deviation from its rightful orientation, or mark. As such, it is a meaningful part of the process of self-discovery and self-creation. In a sense, living is the process of honing our wills so that they can operate within a more appropriate set of options. As we experience more and more of life, the subtleties of our choices and their meanings for us become more apparent. What was yesterday not even something I was aware of may tomorrow become a choice of significant meaning as I begin to journey deeper into the meaning of myself and my interconnections with other people and my world at large. In the same way, forgiveness, which may at first have seemed something that pertained to specific individuals, expands as the reality of my part in the whole becomes more apparent. The early Christians grasped a truth that manifested itself in their symbolic methods of forgiving. To the degree that any individual is less than they can be, then the community as an entity suffers, not just as a result of this specific peccadillo, but because the community's vitality is dependent on the flourishing of the potential of each of its members.

Hearkening back to the anthropology we have articulated reveals that each of us not only comes to the fullness of our existence in the context of the community of the family, but also can only unfold as self-reflexive individuals as a result of the passed-on symbols, images and rituals of our culture, the larger community. Sin, as defined above, is not just an act of will against the divine, but against ourselves as we are called to be and thus against the community of which we are an integral part. To the degree that we cheat, short change, or sidestep our potential selves, we also cheat, short change, and sidestep the communities of which we are part.

St. Thomas Aquinas once used the image of a stained glass window to describe humanity and its inter-relatedness. From a distance, the stained glass window presents the glory of God. Each piece of colored glass is perceived as a unity of incomprehensible beauty. Color plays against color as shape and size add additional dimensions. Aquinas saw the sun that brings to life the stained glass window as God's divine light that shines through the various shades of glass to produce a resplendent pattern of beauty. Each piece of glass is unique. Each piece is made to allow the same glorious light to shine through it in a manner specific to itself, but essential to the whole. Each piece of glass, as each person, has its unique role within the pattern of the window of creation. No piece ranks above or below any other. It is essential that each piece play its specific role and let God shine through it as it was created for.

Beyond this metaphor, we as God's potential images on earth, through the aligning of our wills, allow his radiance to shine through us. This light illumines not just our individual souls, but as importantly, the souls of those we touch. Our authenticity evokes the authenticity of others. Thus, when we sin, when we miss the mark, we limit the light's ability to pass through us. Unlike the metaphor, however, we cause this as a result of our wills, our choices not to be in alignment with God. The forgiveness we ask for is not just the forgiveness of God, but of necessity the forgiveness of the community, which also suffers the lack of our light. Our actions can distort the beauty of creation and thus the whole of creation suffers, not just because of our own small inadequacies, but also because of the light upon which others may be dependent and which we may have denied them. Our actions may have been the source of despair in another or of anger that will turn to cynicism or hatred. The point is that, as human beings, we are tightly linked and the actions we take or omit to take, the attitudes we choose or fail to choose can have ramifications on others far greater than we realize or dare to consider.

Up to this point, we have used quotes from the Bible or from literature as jumping off points or illustrations. Here, I am blessed to be able to share something much more real to enhance this discussion on forgiveness. As of this summer, I never really had the opportunity or the capacity to see many of the aspects of the will to love lived by a real person to such an extent that the incarnation of these ideas pushed by the limits of my intellect to the depths of my heart and soul. I have now been so blessed.

Every year I go away to Cape Cod and stay in a bed and breakfast that over time has become more home than B&B. Every year, most of the people I greet are the same people who have returned often enough to become a kind of family. One year I was given a gift which I was not expecting and for which I was certainly unprepared. On this occasion, someone new came to the house. Before she came, the house owners told us she was coming and that she was struggling with cancer. My first reaction was to be apprehensive. I am not sure about what, but that was my initial response. Before I ever met her, I heard her and what I heard shocked me. I heard the lilt of a laugh and a voice that seemed almost gleeful and childlike. At first I thought that there must be another couple in the house, but then I met the source of that laugh and that voice. To meet this woman was to be first taken aback by the bald head and the luminous eyes and smile, which transformed her into such beauty as to take me aback. My original thoughts had been to be polite and to keep a large space between myself and this person who was struggling with cancer, but my first encounter changed all of that.

It was at breakfast and each of us was eating as more and more members of the house gathered around the table as they woke to a new day. This mesmerizing woman came in and sat across from me. A friend of mine was sitting next to her at the head of the table. Someone got her a cup of coffee from the technical monster that spewed individual cups with grinding complaints as each one was delivered. She then took the cup and placed it almost at the top of her head and began to draw the cup lip down in a straight line; first down her forehead then her nose until it met her lips. The reason for this ritual was that the brain cancer had obliterated her hand eye coordination. I believe she did this once, and from that point on the friend of mine, unbidden, would raise the cup to her lips and then the spoon filled with fruit and yogurt. She merely thanked him as if he had picked up a dropped napkin.

As people talked, she fully participated, and the complete joy and happiness of each moment seemed to spill from her in both sound and spirit. I was later to learn that she was dying. In fact, she was desperately fighting for each moment and each day. She had begun this journey a while ago with a brain tumor that had tentacles, which slowly invaded her brain. At this point she was covered with the patches that enable relief from extensive pain over time. Later, I was to find out that the cancer had now invaded her bones and her liver. These patches were to relieve her of the constant pain from the bone cancer. Not once did I see anything about her countenance which revealed anything but complete joy in being alive and being where she was.

But why would one mention this experience in the middle of a section on forgiveness? Forgiveness is not merely a stance that one can choose toward one who offends; it is as much a stance one must choose toward oneself. The peace, joy, and love that emanated from this incredible woman could never have issued from a soul burdened with self-pity, self-loathing, or preoccupation and disappointment. Who she is reflected a soul that had forgiven her body for its cruel treachery. She was humble in her weakness, yet not burdened by it. She never demanded because she still had the courage to let the gifts of life surprise her. She was oriented toward life in all its wonder and not curled inward in what would have been an understandable self-preoccupation or focus. She participated in everything to her best ability and reveled in the wonder and happiness of those with whom she shared any event.

Forgiveness starts with ourselves and our ability to accept who we are, as well as who we can be. Certainly, this wonderful manifestation of the human spirit with her vast capacity of the human heart and will was not only special, but unique and grace-filled. Most of us know our flaws, our inadequacies, our imperfections with fine-pointed awareness. For many of us, these act as limitations to what we will allow ourselves to experience. Primal forgiveness is, in part, the active embracing of these realizations and the insecurities they can engender. This dear woman had not only done this with the reality of herself as she was in the fullness of health, but then again as her body slowly betrayed her. Only when we have come to this internal self-acceptance and the forgiveness that allows us to embrace our shortcomings can we be truly free to experience the fullness of life and its wonders.

Forgiveness is thus not an act of an individual in power standing over another individual stooped in remorse. Forgiveness is a balm provided by the forgiver out of the abundance of the reserves of having been already forgiven, both by ourselves and by the other we seek to imitate. Forgiveness is the only ointment that can heal the soul of humanity. This ointment comes not from a priestly caste and their ability to commune with the divine, but from our common need to will ourselves into being through the deliberate choices of meaning that we make at each moment of our lives and the actions that we take which follow from them. This shared radical responsibility and accountability, with its constant call to self-honesty and humility, is the creative source of such an ointment. Forgiveness, far from being a posture of power, is the great humbler. It is the supreme act of the will to love, for it is an act of the self truly acknowledging the subjectivity of the self and/or the individual before it with empathy, generosity, and respect. It is the fruit of self-awareness and the blessing of having been loved and forgiven by another.

The Will to Love and the Purposeful Life

The will to love has been presented as essential to human life. The will, as the primal source of human agency, action, and power has been revealed in the shared gift of the loving creator for this unique being called human. It is not in the sole act of the labor of birth that we are created, but in the infinity of choices that follow, which make manifest the unique human person we create.

The concept of the will to love has been the direct and undaunted desire to place this potential, this power, within its rightful context. We have taken this life force, the will, and given it an object, love, in order to discern whether this object is rich enough and proper to the vitality it would seek to express, direct and nurture for its own betterment and for that of the world which is woven inextricably into it. The object of the will is love, not the highly charged emotional love of romantic novels and Hollywood movies, but the more mature and conscious reality, which forces open our closed hearts, demands the transformation of our fear into hope, and diminishes our egoism in its outward trajectory. It is love that illuminates our interconnectedness, our oneness as a species. It is a love that is immense when it is lowly, invincible when it is vulnerable, and ever renewed in its being poured forth. This love is fed by the light that comes from being attuned to the other. It is the generosity that originates from being attuned to the world that evokes the possibility of our wills to love and thus transform ourselves and those around us.

As a result of this interplay between will and love, each human being must be appreciated not as a static object, but rather as a being on a journey. Each moment along the way carries with it the opportunity to move between possibility and actuality. Who we are never stops being created for as long as our journeys on this earth continue. Every step along the way of our unique journeys will both evoke and expose opportunities and the realities formed from the ramifications of our previous free choices. Each act of will has the potential to express our love and thus nurture or starve the individuals which we are. In this way, the whole of human existence has as its goal the will's ultimate expression in bringing love to the self from which our will operates, to the world in which its object, love, can engender life.

A related thread that consistently weaves throughout this work is that of unity. This unity is at the core of humanity and the world of which humanity is a part. This unity has called into question the division of reality into subjects and objects, by holding firmly that one cannot exist without the other. It has also uncompromisingly declared that the ongoing dialogue of the self with the other is not only mutually constitutive, but necessary to the existence of both. The mystery of the other that can never be resolved and the same mystery at the core of our very selves. This basic stance throws into question our entire concept of the "apotheosis of individuality" as an isolated autonomous ego, forever alone with its own ideas, thoughts, desires, feelings, fears, and hopes. In contradistinction to this popular conception of the individual, the self is constituted in and through relationship.

As a fundamental key to the melding of the will to love and the anthropology presented here is the distinction between the notions of freedom as liberty, with its focus on external choices, and freedom as the capacity to choose the meanings of who we are and the events of our lives. We have consistently rejected the primacy of the externality of freedom as the true seat of human creativity, agency, or will. We have accepted the fact that external events are beyond our control and that if we were to place our definition of freedom in external choices, we would be confronted by the absurdity of life. It is our capacity to will the meanings of our experiences and choices that shape who we are and the world we live in. These meanings are primary and preactive, and thus the basis for how we experience, as well as what we respond to, within our lives. In this sense our capacity to choose these meanings is expressive of our creativity and determinative of who we really are and the lives that we will lead.

Within the context of "The Will to Love" the question of the purpose of human life is essential to grasp if one is truly to appreciate how these various facets of human existence intertwine. At the very beginning of this journey, we stated one purpose, and that was to love and serve our God with all our hearts and soul. At a very abstract level, it would be fair to say that the idea of the will to love is the response to the question of the purpose of life. To leave this answer of the purpose-filled life at the level of "loving God and our neighbor with all our heart and soul" is true, but still too abstract. The concept of the "a purpose-filled life" traditionally has focused on trying to see behind any specific individual life and ascertain what would make life worthy of all our capacities and capabilities regardless of any specific lived experience. The question of the purposeful life has always needed to battle the realities of death and suffering and the many tragedies possible within the course of one's existence. In this respect, it is a question asked outside of the limitations or gifts of any specific individual, born at any time to any culture or creed. This kind of question is overarching and not a particularly popular kind of questioning in modern culture.

The question of the purpose of an individual's life and, more generically, of human life in general will always hinge on the view one has of human existence. The same might be said about any other creature, such as my dog, Harry. I would probably be the first to admit that the purpose of Harry's life is simply in his living. The idea of Harry as a creature, who seeks to be fed, sheltered and part of a pack all makes sense. Harry's life would be very fulfilled by ensuring that these basic concerns are addressed. If Harry were not fixed, he would also have, as part of his menu of facets of his purposeful existence the proliferation of his life through the creation of puppies. Few of us would argue with the above. Few of us would not grasp the innate aspects of purpose within Harry. Nature and the expression of purpose through instinct are very clear in the creatures with which we share this world.

When one turns one's attention from Harry to humanity, one has to ask oneself if there really is a significant difference in these two kinds of existence. In other words, how far is humanity from the instinctual laws that permeate all life? The answer to this question is not as clear as one might think. With the advent of modern science and its continued abilities to peer deeper into our bodies and study how we operate and thus how to intervene when our operations go awry, a view of humanity as a complex machine, has become more feasible to many. This view that high-level human functions can be explained by looking at our bodies is called materialistic reductionism. Its fundamental tenet is that most, if not all, human experiences can be tracked and explained by referring to the complexity of our physical beings. Modern scientists believe they have found the cause of certain cancers in the workings of stem cells. Neurologists have created topographies of the human brain that show where the centers for speech, memory, analytical, and poetic thinking reside. Vast numbers of diseases have been slowed down or eradicated through our understanding of immunology. All of this renders the idea of material reductionism less absurd than we once thought. Many scientists believe that one day we will be able to predict with incredible accuracy many aspects of a person's life by our understanding of their DNA. We might be able to know years before any symptoms make themselves known that John will get Alzheimer's and be able to stop it. We might be able to know a person's sexual preference long before she becomes sexually mature. What does this all mean?

First of all, being able to identify the cause of something does not mean one has discovered the thing in itself. We have acknowledged that humans are physical beings. What we have never accepted is that our physical beings are expressive of our complete identities and capacities. The reductionist view we just discussed, as is often the case is not wrong, rather it is incomplete. For humanity has more than one modality of being. A modality is here being used to describe an essential facet of our natures that not only makes us different from my dog Harry, but also much more complex than the material reductionists would like to admit. Our physicality is as real as the non-physical aspects of our beings. It would be absurd to not acknowledge the very real aspects of our beings that are material and that follow the laws appropriate to all material elements within nature. The question is whether this view is broad enough to explain the full breadth of who we are.

There are many thinkers, within the sciences and medicine in particular who will not accept a reductionist and materialistic view of the person as a complete explanation of who we are. At the same time, many who hold dearly to the fact that humans are much more than complex machines are also loathe to accept the once-prevalent notion of the human being as comprised of two vastly different elements, body and soul. This dualism has been present for centuries and still lurks around intellectual corners, be they theological or philosophical. In response to both extremes, there is another group of people who recognize the multifaceted aspects of human beings but refuse to divide them and thus accept these various facets of being human as a unity. Just as one can discuss many things from various perspectives, these thinkers hold that looking at an individual and focusing on the material facets of his being is just as real as looking at that same human and focusing on his mental capabilities or his emotional or spiritual facets. This is a non-reductionist, non-materialist view of humanity that considers the idea of finding a spirit without a body a concept beyond the intelligible limits of thought. The concept of the person that emerges from this unified perspective is based on a notion of humanity that is inherently relational.

The will to love is a framework for describing the human being from multiple vantage points. We have discovered the veracity of the self as a unique interaction between the situatedness of our physical beings, the creative transcendence of our mental capacities, and the vivifying force of our spirits, which inform and transcend the whole. This notion of the person is yet another hearkening back to how we humans are images of our Creator as the supreme archetype. The notion of the triune God, which is a complex mystery, is given clarity as we more fully appreciate our humanity as being composed of multiple modalities existing as a unified reality. This view of the person reinforces the anthropology which appreciates each individual as a community and the notion of relationship as the first principle in understanding the human person. This position manifests the reality that, fundamentally, humans have a relational nature and that understanding this is key to understanding the centrality of the will to love at the heart of who we are. Illustratively, even simple living things, such as plants, have natures that are the sources of their need to fulfill the laws of their existences. The parable of the fig tree told in the New Testament to evoke our understanding of the greater vocation of human nature and its integration with human will is a beautiful example of how recognition of nature's laws unfolding in a fig tree, which cannot participate in its outcomes, is but a pale reminder of both our capacity and responsibility to fulfill our natures.

> A man had a fig tree planted in his vineyard; and he came seeking fruit on it and found none. And he said to the vinedresser, "Lo,

these three years I have come seeking fruit on this fig tree, and I find none. Cut it down; why should it use up the ground?" And he answered him, "Let it alone, sir, this year also, till I dig about it and put on manure. And if it bears fruit next year, well and good; but if not, you can cut it down"

Luke 13:6–10 (RSV)

Here, the vinedresser appeals to the owner of the garden to give him another year to coax the expected fruit from the barren fig tree. It is clear that a fig tree that cannot fulfill its purpose, which is to produce figs, is not worth the space it occupies within the garden. In telling this parable, Jesus is using this myth to place in juxtaposition the fig tree, which lacks internal will, and humanity, imbued with not just a will, but a free, unconstrained one that is central to our achieving our purposes and fulfillment. The tree can do nothing of itself to rectify the situation, so the vinedresser intercedes on its behalf. We, however, are creatures who can and must will our actualization. The question thus remains, what is the fulfillment or purpose of the human person?

At the very start of this reflection, the creation myth from Genesis spoke of humanity as a potential image of God. In this statement is a key to what our natures are capable of and how we must participate in their fulfillment. Genesis is the story of creation, the articulation of God's nature as creator and life giver. Genesis also reveals that God's creative nature expresses his love, his generativity, and his unhindered capacity to will. One could conceive of a god who chose to exist in simple self-satisfied completeness, never moving beyond his own being. The God we seek to know and who is the author and sustainer of all that is, is not self-contained. The generativity and creative outpouring expresses the essence of the Being that we have come to call Father. This term has never been a term denoting gender, but a term expressive of relationship. So much nonsense has been focused on God's supposed masculinity without the profound realization of the fact that this moniker of relationship is another expression of the core of being itself, which is relational. As potential images of God, we share these aspects of his nature; we are first and foremost beings in relationship. Our genders are expressive of the creative facets of the One who is Father, Spirit Mother, and Son. Our natures, like his, are thus outward-facing, creative, capable of willing and incomplete without the expression or experience of love.

We are also rational as God is rational, for this rationality is expressed in and through the wonder of the natural laws that permeate our universe, as well as our very selves. The creativity of God is also a call within us to be creative as he is creative through continuing our species, enhancing our existence with music, art, poetry, and dance, and most notably through the giving of life by our willed choice to share our lives. It is through the many ways that we can and do share our lives with each other that we have the potential to make each other whole and heal the many wounds that burden our souls. Like the fig tree, if a created thing does not give expression to its purpose as expressed within the natural laws that drive it, it is useless. For humans with independent wills, giving expression to our natures involves more than just letting the natural laws that control our physical beings follow their course and create figs, so to speak.

A life of purpose is not some antiquated concept; it is the proper object of our existence. Certainly, happiness is wonderful when we are graced with it. Joy is equally a gem to be cherished, but these are not the goals of our existence, and if we believe they are we are certainly being set up for disappointment. These are the symptoms of the paths that we are choosing that are expressing the fullness of our beings, but they are not the end in themselves. The purposeful life is a life in which I can discover myself and my world, and in which I can bring that miraculous discovery to myself and to others through the exercise of all aspects of my being. The will to love is thus not a quaint idea or a nice slogan; it is the orientation and practice that has as its goal the purposeful life we all seek from within the depths of our selves. In the New Testament, Jesus defines love very specifically as clear acts of selfless generosity that are imitative of the kind of love bestowed on each of us by God.

> Love your enemies, do good to those who hate you, bless those who curse you, pray for those who abuse you. To him who strikes you on the cheek, offer the other also; and from him who takes away your coat do not withhold even your shirt. Give to everyone who begs from you; and of him who takes away your goods do not ask again. And as you wish that men would do to you, do so to them... for He is kind to the ungrateful and the selfish. Be merciful even as your father is merciful.
> Luke 6:27–31, 35–36

This self-giving, that is true life, which is the most fundamental characteristic of the purpose-filled life, is expressed in the orientation of the person's will outward toward the world (people, places, things, situations), in which the person both finds him- or herself and discovers the other. It is a posture of generosity. It is consistent with the previous descriptions of the authentic interaction of the self and the other. It is the outward trajectory of the self's awareness, energy, and orientation, as well as the alignment of our will to respond to what life brings us by doing the good that is within our power. This orientation of interacting with the world, of being attuned to and opened to the other, as other, and having the generosity to respond to the other in love is at the core of the meaning of human life. It is also in imitation of the nature of God's love for each of us, which is generous and kind, even when we are undeserving. Withholding and turning inward as acts of fear, stinginess, and smallness of spirit are real options for us as humans, but they are choices of death over life. This death is not just of the individual who wills these postures, but also of the world from whom these lives have been taken and the real loss to all whose lives are reduced by the unique and un-repeatable self who chooses to withhold. We are all lessened and perverted through inauthentic acts of being that poison the very fabric of the community.

The first and the greatest marker of the good life is peace. It is an inner peace that illuminates within the core of the individual independent of her external dispositions or agitations or distractions. It is the last gift that Jesus was to give us before he left this world: "Peace I leave with you, my peace I give unto you: not as the world giveth, give I unto you. Let not your heart be troubled, neither let it be afraid" (John 14:27). This peace is the marker that informs one that he has met a very special person. It is not often an easy thing to perceive. It is not the Hollywood-like disassociated floating and lack of focus; it is not always restful or pious. It does not break the unique characteristics of the individuals it graces. In a world distracted by externals, it is often missed as it lurks deep within as the bedrock of how one is attuned to life and its calls. Peace is in part the lack of the warring of the many dimensions of our beings, but it may also be the instigator of the stretching of our faculties resulting from the still soft voice that calls us to face even deeper levels of our fear. Often the images imbedded within each of us by the cultures we live within can make us deaf to our own inner peace, as well as that of others. The discipline of listening and the additional capacity to hear and then to dwell are essential to refining our attentiveness to the discovery of this most exotic of jewels. Once discovered, peace will captivate the discoverer, and he will thirst for more and it will blossom as it leads anyone longing to dwell with her to her source.

Markers of Avoiding the Purpose Filled Life

As was said previously, but is worth repeating, humans often learn the hardest lessons through negative experiences. In our desire to live a purposeful life, it is therefore, illustrative to describe a few of the indicators one may run up against that may be indicative of the reality that one is on the wrong path. The following descriptions are meant to paint pictures of both how we as a community and as individuals can miss the call to the fullness of life and thus a life that is inherently purposeful.

Anyone who lives near a large city or who travels a lot may have noticed a phenomenon becoming far too common and that is indicative of the opposite of many of the elements of the full rich life that is at the heart of the purposeful life. This phenomenon is the ability of men and women to shut themselves off from their fellow "human beings" by turning off their senses. This phenomenon is particularly apparent in large cities such as New York where people no longer meet the eyes of each other on the subway or sidewalk. Not only is there a decreased ease in meeting each other's eyes, or dare it happen, offering a smile or a hello; but if this does happen and we happen to become aware of someone in need, the ability to completely shut down our sensory apparatus seems to have reached new heights. Countless times a day men and women who would consider themselves sensitive and caring people walk by other human beings laying on the cold pavement covered only with a thin blanket in freezing weather, rain, snow, and every other condition nature can offer. This ability to move through life with blinders on and to turn what appears to be a blind eye to such suffering would elicit a multitude of reasons if one were to ask those who actually pass the person cold and hungry. The question is what is behind both our individual ability to become de-sensitized and the community's same capacity?

The two most basic factors behind this phenomenon are fear and despair. To make this even more problematic, technology has gone far in providing us tools for isolating our senses from the world and the world from us through iPods and the music they can pipe into our heads, or the cell phones and Blackberries that allow us to keep our eyes lowered and our attention carefully focused. Don't miss-perceive what is being stated. Music is wonderful; it is the non-verbal sound of love, concern, and of the eternal echoes of life. The issue is not the music, but its capacity to shut out the world and the lives within it. The issue is the desensitizing of humans to life, to the many dimensions of being, such as suffering, rejoicing, praying, dancing. It is not the iPod or the music, but whether it is being used to shut life out or actually bring life to us in its fullest? It is the same with the newspaper, Blackberry, and cell phone. In and of themselves they are not the issues. They do require us to pause and to ask ourselves what role they play in our unending call to respond to life, to be attuned to our existence and of those around us. When are these goods potentially being used in ways that enable us to lessen our ability to hear the call at our very centers to live as well as to will to love? If we truly discover ourselves in the ongoing process of hearing and responding to the other, what if any role are these devices and our addiction to them adding or taking from this necessary dialogue? Once again it is not the "what" that is pivotal, but the "how" and the "why." Even the awareness of our need to listen, to be attuned and to be able to hear, which we have clearly articulated as skills that must be practiced and developed, are placed in jeopardy as we run from what we may see, stuff noise in our ears so there is little chance that we may hear the moan of another or even worse the call to give of ourselves.

Fear and despair are critical to our discussion of living the purposeful life and our continued quest for the fundamental characteristics of authentic personhood, because fear and despair are dimensions of retracted existence, shutting the world out and a turning in. They are in fact the signs that life, as meant for each of us, is being blocked. Fear causes the authentic self to close itself off from the world through inauthentic interactions that involve masking its true vulnerability by way of manipulation of both itself and the other. A fear-based stance cannot accept the other as truly other for the self is in a constant state of dread; a dread that the self will be discovered and be found wanting, and simultaneously a dread that I will never be discovered and thus always be isolated and empty. At the core of this fear and the dread it engenders is the self's experience of a personal lack of meaning and identity and a true horror that this emptiness that one is will swallow one up for eternity.

Fear, at its heart, is born of our desire to control and to protect ourselves as well as those we love. In this sense as with most things, fear is not bad or evil. It is what we do with our fear that is of interest. We cannot control life. We cannot control anything really. This means that we have to embrace the mystery of the unfolding of life and respond authentically to what it brings to our doorsteps. Fear and its tight linkage to suffering are dimensions of life that we must embrace; once embraced we can do more to share, alleviate, and embrace another's suffering than we ever thought possible. In this reorientation of our energy away from removing what cannot be removed or eradicating what we cannot; we can now put our life forces and our wills in focus on how we can participate in these difficult experiences such that we can give relief, hope, and strength to those who are most in need of it. Fear is the clear marker of where we are loath to go and where we are unwilling to dwell. The faith that believes there is no place in which God's life-giving love and light can go is the only remedy to our fears.

If not faced, fear can lead to the most destructive choice that humans can choose, and that is despair. It is this despair that immobilizes the self from taking any action to enter and participate in life's situations. The posture of despair convinces the self that there is nothing to be done; there are no actions that can be taken. Fear isolates, despair immobilizes. Fear and despair are not just pathologies of individuals; they are also pathologies of societies, governments, religious institutions, corporations, and cultures in general. Despair takes fear to a level where one chooses isolation rather than life and all the potential options that life offers cease to exist. Despair is the loss of the self and a dislocation of the self from life. Despair says that there is not light and that no light will ever be able to penetrate the darkness that I am experiencing. It is the complete willed choice to completely turn away from existence, rather than face the reality that we cannot protect ourselves or each other. Out of our primal desire to live, the person who chooses despair chooses death. The only way out of this spiral is to be forced back into life. One in despair must be made to reopen their eyes and ears and taste the life that is beckoning to them. Helping one move from despair back to hope and faith is the greatest gift one person can give to another. It is a costly gift and most certainly a prime example of the will to love.

Many societies today are enveloped by fear and despair. Its signposts are almost everywhere. Listen to the many political speeches being made in America; regardless of their specific content, how many are poised to evoke our collective fear? We see this in the rhetoric used in foreign policies that refer to "evil empires," "axis of evil," that refer to wars as "crusades." In our social policies, one can hear the fear driven rhetoric which often claims that if "X" or "Y" occurs, our families or marriage as sacred institutions will be destroyed. Regardless of what is being discussed, the method of presentation is appealing to our collective fear.

Often fear is closely coupled with exclusion or restricting another's freedoms. Fear is one of the most effective tools used to keep our hearts and minds closed. Fear has been used to support segregation, to attempt to restrict the expansion of the vote, to attempt to make inter-racial marriage illegal, and it continues as the force behind many major social issues today. How many hate crimes happen every year because people fear what they do not understand or know? Even in our churches we can hear religious leaders railing from their pulpits against this and that, trying to instill fear as a method for controlling. Fear and despair are the foundations of isolation, exclusion, despair, and death of the spirit. They are the antithesis of the characteristics of the purposeful life. They are important, therefore, because they can illuminate their opposites, which are the foundations of living the good life, which each human being is called to.

Fear and despair stand in direct counterdistinction to two central dispositions basic to not only a will to love and authentic existence, but also to a Christian orientation to the world. The two basic orientations of the authentic human as well as the professed Christian are faith and hope. These two characteristics are also two key markers for those seeking to live the purposeful life. Where fear isolates based on despair, faith creates the space for the discovery and awe of myself and the other as loved and as infinite possibility. Loved first as I am, both by the other in whom and through whom I discover myself existentially, as well as through the Other who manifests himself to me as the larger creative and sustaining love that encapsulates and calls forth the self that I am and the world of which I am an integral piece.

Hope is the second critical aspect of this dynamic for faith creates the space and hope, its proper object. Hope provides the proper disposition of humble openness to the fact that no individual is determined by their past, their physical make up, and their particular place in time or society. Hope acknowledges that nothing is determined but what each of us wills to be so. God created man to love him and in so doing gave humanity a will to choose. God also created humanity with the potential to be like him. By so doing God gave humanity a pattern to follow. He told humanity that he, God, was the Archetype and we were to be his images. He told us that he gave us wills to achieve this end. In the fullness of time, he sent his son, Jesus, who consistently proclaimed that he was here to do his Father's bidding. He was the perfect image of God the Archetype, and he called us to follow him. Faith is the necessary condition for hope. Together, faith and hope make possible love. Without faith and hope love cannot be present as it has been defined herein. Faith creates the space for the other to be other and for the self to be exposed and discovered. Hope is what keeps the arms of Christ from being closed.

The New Testament is filled with additional markers to the purposeful life that are not particularly unique to Christianity but continue to express the truths that underlie so many faiths. The ability to understand the place of suffering in life is critical to living the purposeful life. Not only Christianity, but Judaism and Buddhism have been clear that humanity must accept suffering as a part of life. It is our lot to be molded not just by the sweet nectar of the fig or the honeycomb but also through bitter herbs and unleavened bread. Claiming that suffering should be sought after and revered is absurd; rather, it should be seen as natural as the light of the sun is to the glow of the moon. It is, unfortunately, in the sufferings of our lives that we most often discover ourselves, for it is when we are passive, which is the root of the word for suffering in Latin, that we are most open to discovering the source of our being and the possibility of awakening to deeper levels of our existence. It is often surprising how many Christians have lost their faith due to some horrible trauma in their life. Jesus came to earth as the unique mystery of humanity and divinity combined. His life was filled with many moments of joy, sorrow, and excruciating pain. As his followers, how can we expect anything less? Mary, his mother, who gave her unflinching *fiat* to God, at no small price followed her son and bore a mother's suffering as she watched her son scorned, rejected, abandoned, and then maltreated and killed.

In short, throughout this reflection multiple characteristics of the purposeful life or the life lived authentically have been mentioned. Some key markers that were highlighted are central to this journey each of us is on. By keeping them close to our minds and to our consciousness maybe they can act as the as spiritual signposts and therefore opportunities for correcting our paths as we move forward.

Soil and Spirit

One of the most fundamental twists in human existence is the simultaneous awareness that as humans we are both soil and soul. We are both grounded in our situatedness in time and place, in our integrated natures as earthly dust and transcendent spirit. It is this rootedness or, put another way, our imbedded nature that both makes us another face of nature's wonders and full participants in nature's cycles, power, fury, and beauty. As such, we are capable of both willing great acts of courage, selflessness, and love and simultaneously of manifesting unfathomable distortion, evil, and sin. It is important for us to discover those who have gone before us and have manifested the full wonder of our capacities. In this way we are forced to remember not just the negative aspects that we hear so much about, but more importantly the wonder that is ours to be and to pour forth onto our world.

During the Second World War many innocent people were brutally murdered and placed in work camps purely based on their religion, their nationality, ethnicity, sexual orientation, or as a result of stepping in and attempting to help victims. The Germans were often brutal, both in their use of prisoners to control prisoners and there callous acts of cruelty. As described in gripping detail in a book entitled *I*

Was Dr. Mengele's Assistant, the ability of the prison officials to set up a structure of control and rewards based on the psychological terror and hopelessness of the prisoners enabled the Germans to use the captives for gathering information, managing the actual mass killings, and the ultimate disposal of the bodies in the notorious gas chambers.

Attempted escapes from these work camps were unacceptable events. It threatened the reputation of the officers in control as well as the lower level German soldiers responsible for maintaining order and output. To ensure that these incidents were few and far between many camps had policies of deterrence that if a prisoner escaped or attempted to escape, another prisoner or group of prisoners from their barracks would be randomly selected and killed. Some camps shot this person or persons; some placed the randomly selected into a starvation hut, where they would slowly die of the elements and a lack of food and water. This horrible method of minimizing escapes or their attempts were extremely successful as the other prisoners were left to hear the agony of those men starving day and night. Many claimed that it was the slow reduction in sound that haunted them the most as they were helpless to intervene.

In 1941 a prisoner escaped Auschwitz. The commandant's policy was quite specific; if this occurred, ten randomly selected prisoners from the same block would be placed into a starvation hut as the escapee and their comrades would be forced to listen to the daily agony of their merciless deaths. On one particular day, ten men were being pulled from the line because one of their cell mates had escaped. One of the ten selected to die, Franciszek Gajowniczek, began to cry: "My wife! My children! I will never see them again!" Certainly this fact was true for many, but on this particular day, prisoner 16670, a Polish priest by the name of Maximilian Kolbe, stepped forward and requested to take this man's place. The guards were astonished and decided to let this foolish man get his request and led the prisoner to the starvation hut with his nine unlucky compatriots. This incredible act of self-sacrifice offered for a stranger reflected how deeply Fr.

Kolbe was willing to love and to what cost to himself. The ten men who were to share this starvation hut were also to discover that this act of love was not random or isolated, but a consistent facet of this man's being. As the days progressed, Kolbe ministered to the men, and he watched as the majority died in pitiful agony. Finally, with only two remaining and Fr. Kolbe still singing hymns and praying aloud, the guards entered and gave him a lethal shot of carbolic acid.

This polish priest is an example of someone who truly lived the will to love. His final generous act was possible because he had embraced a way of living his life and of seeing his world and the people in it that he was to live day in and day out. Such unfathomable acts of personal sacrifice do not just emerge randomly. They bespeak innumerable smaller acts of love, of generosity, and of being attuned to life. Father Kolbe was made a saint on October 10, 1982. What is important to remember is that Maximilian Kolbe was just a man. What made him extraordinary was how he chose to live. There are many men and women of incredible courage, generosity, valor, hope, and virtue living today as well in the past. These men and women offer us a constant reminder of our calls and our capabilities.

No matter what the situation, the pattern of love and the embracing of the subject as the one who failed us in some way is the call of each of us in our lives. The outcomes of our acts of love, are never assured, nor are these the point. It is the action of loving the one in need, who seeks wholeness, which is the objective. Many of us have reason to have mixed feelings about our church, i.e. the human manifestation of her spiritual perfection, in response to how it has let us down or, in some cases, actually caused us pain and suffering. Everywhere we find hate, animosity, loathing, or just raw pain, we are called to discover how through individual acts of love we can embrace these souls, so that the souls of those who suffer may be free. In all the cases where we have described real suffering, injustice, and horrific actions, we have touched the soil of our lives. Only our will to love can transform the soil into life-giving spirit, not by eradicating what happened, but by transcending it. This step of willing human acceptance and empathy to co-exist with our belief and faith is enabling the light of life to reemerge in places permeated by darkness, or as Jesus put it:

> For every one who does evil hates the light, and does not come to the light, lest his deeds should be exposed. But he who does what is true comes to the light, that it may be clearly seen that his deeds have been wrought in God.
> John 3: 20–21, (RSV)

In the book of Job, the author speaks quite openly about the role of darkness is the life of those who do evil for evil's sake as well as those who do it under the misdirection of righteousness.

> There are those who rebel against the light, who are not acquainted with its ways, and do not stay in its paths...The eye of the adulterer also waits for the twilight, saying, 'No eye will see me,' and he disguises his face... For deep darkness in morning for all of them; for they are friends with the terrors of deep darkness.
> Job 24: 13, 15, 17 (RSV)

Job grasps a universal truth that evil abhors light as it abhors its true reflection. Faith, hope, and their flower, love, are and will always be the only possible methods to transcend these awful human events. To complete this list of requisite elements is, of course, the human will. If I choose to wallow in human suffering and misdeeds, no one will be able to force light where darkness is chosen. One of the many benefits of solid psychotherapy is to be able to slowly enable one to let go of the apparent security, predictability, and control of choosing darkness, even with its isolation and alienation, and to slowly let back in life's light into their world.

Based on the entire view of humanity and the spirituality that is possible and compatible with this foundation, which we have thoughtfully pondered over, we are left with many puzzles. Much of this reflection has focused on rebuilding humanity from the very ground of our human purpose to our unique way of being in our world as the only creatures who are, by their very nature, self creative and other creative. In other words, we are the only creatures so equipped to be able to co-redeem this world in partnership with each other and God. Indirectly, this reflection has accused humanity of abandoning its purpose, its responsibility, and its ultimate accountability as each individual alone, as individuals in relation to each other, and ultimately as persons in relation to the world for which they were originally created. The actual toll of this abdication has already begun to show itself at the edges, which are becoming frayed and already manifest very real symptoms on our planet, in our societies, homes, and even our own persons.

Another aspect of this fraying was magnificently articulated hundreds of years ago in Dickens's *Christmas Carol*.

> Forgive me if I am not justified in what I ask,' said Scrooge, looking intently at the Spirit's robe,' but I see something strange, and not belonging to yourself, protruding from your skirts. Is it a foot or a claw.'
> 'It might be a claw, for the flesh there is upon it,' was the Spirit's sorrowful reply. 'Look here.'
> From the foldings of its robe, it brought two children; wretched, abject, frightful, hideous, miserable. They knelt down at its feet, and clung upon the outside of its garment.
> 'Oh, Man. look here. Look, look, down here.' exclaimed the Ghost.
> They were a boy and a girl. Yellow, meager, ragged, scowling, wolfish; but prostrate, too, in their humility. Where graceful youth should have filled their features out, and touched them with its freshest tints, a stale and shriveled hand, like that of age, had pinched, and twisted them, and pulled them into shreds. Where angels might have sat enthroned, devils lurked, and

glared out menacing. No change, no degradation, no perversion of humanity, in any grade, through all the mysteries of wonderful creation, has monsters half so horrible and dread.

Scrooge started back, appalled. Having them shown to him in this way, he tried to say they were fine children, but the words choked themselves, rather than be parties to a lie of such enormous magnitude.

'Spirit, are they yours.' Scrooge could say no more.

'They are Man's,' said the Spirit, looking down upon them. 'And they cling to me, appealing from their fathers. This boy is Ignorance. This girl is Want. Beware them both, and all of their degree, but most of all beware this boy, for on his brow I see that written which is Doom, unless the writing be erased. Deny it.' cried the Spirit, stretching out its hand towards the city. 'Slander those who tell it ye. Admit it for your factious purposes, and make it worse. And abide the end.

—A Christmas Carol, Stave 3:
The Second of the Three Spirits

To take the author's point a step further from the line of thought we have been focused on, Dickens foresaw the outcome of unbridled capitalism as the confusion, at all levels of society, between need and want. When those that have the means cannot truly grasp the huge distinction between a need and a want, at the level of society, it is as if the ship has no rudder. Our morality becomes foundationless. What is acceptable and unacceptable becomes a spectrum that is too large to accept as a moral spectrum at all. We find this exists in most Western large cities of our century; unfathomable wealth and dire poverty living side by side. We find garbage tins filled each night with the scraps from rich men's tables to rot on the curb, while soup kitchens stretch every bean to feed the huge numbers of needy. In many ways these two worlds exist in parallel. To give the devil his due, many give to charities. Nonetheless this situation does not merely persist but worsens as humanity becomes less appalled at what it sees, to say nothing of what is happening around the globe. Jesus told a parable of such a world, though one wonders if he could have imagined the escalation of his image.

> There was a rich man who was clothed in purple and fine linen and who feasted sumptuously every day. And at his gate lay a poor man named Lazarus, full of sores, who desired to be fed with what fell from the rich man's table; moreover the dogs came and licked his sores. The poor man died and was carried by the angels to Abraham's bosom. The rich man also died and was buried; and in Hades, being tormented, he lifted up his eyes, and saw Abraham far off and Lazarus in his bosom. And he called out, 'Father Abraham, have mercy upon me, and send Lazarus to dip the end of his finger in water and cool my tongue; for I am in anguish in this flame.' But Abraham said, 'Son, remember that you in your lifetime received your good things, and Lazarus in like manner evil things; but now he is comforted here, and you are in anguish. And besides all this, between us and you a great chasm has been fixed, in order that those who would pass from here to you may not be able, and none may cross from there to us.'
> Luke 16:19–26 (RSV)

This parable and Dickens's *Christmas Carol* share a common theme. In both stories the intercessor, Jacob Marley and Lazarus, are both kept from interfering in the sufferings of humanity once their lives have been spent. For Jacob and the rich man it is part of their torment. When a society encumbered more with poverty than wealth has this same confusion between need and want, the confusion becomes catastrophic. As a result of mass media, entire segments of the world still without hot water in their homes or still subsisting are now being flooded with images of mass material abundance. This raises rightful expectations that if I am willing to learn and labor such as these wealthy people, why do we not share, at least, in their abundance? Is an individual with a net worth of in excess of

$100MM not a moral issue in a world where there are billions who barely survive day by day?

So what is to be done and by whom? I believe this reflection necessitates that the answer is clear; each of us must be willing to love as our way of being and to do the good that we are called to do, regardless of one's creed, ethnic background, nationality, or any other spurious excluder. This reflection has contained within it many recommendations for human consideration. In closing, the primary call to action that emerges from this reflection is that we must alter the focus of modern education from merely providing us the skills to acquire, to a curriculum centered on conveying the miracle of who we are to our children, young boys and girls and the men and women that make it to the university. If we do not continue to drive home to ourselves and our young who they are, what their capacities are, and what their responsibilities are to themselves, their neighbor, and their world, we will not be successful in saving our world or ourselves.

As long as the sun still shines and we have breath in our lungs, we can change the world by doing only one thing, and that is changing ourselves. That has been the core message of this reflection. This is not impossible, nor is it overwhelming in its call. In fact, what makes this so hard is that it is so simple.

If we want to teach our children we are matter, I promise you they will not disappoint and they will act more like beasts than men. This reflection has opened up the question of who we are and what are we are capable of; its answers have been made abundantly clear; we are sons and daughters of God. What we are capable of is a mixture of our wills and our capacities. We must will our capacities into life. We must be willing to embrace life and to develop our ability to be attuned to it. Once we discover we are alive and we are "little less than the angels," we must choose the path of *The Will to Love*. Nothing more is needed.

Conclusion

In an effort to close this reflection in a manner simple yet profound in articulating the central message of the meaning of the *Will to Love* the distant words of St. Teresa of Avilla provide our final reflection. St. Teresa gave this poignant and brief instruction to her nuns in the sixteenth century. This instruction continues to be as relevant today as then. When all the ideas of this reflection fade from your mind her simple devotion, which resounds in these few lines, will always spark the truth most critical to our future as fellow human beings and as Christians.

> Christ has no body now on earth, but yours;
> no hands, but yours;
> no feet, but yours.
> It is your eyes through which
> Christ's compassion looks out to the world;
> your feet with which he must walk about doing good;
> your hands with which he blesses humanity;
> your voice with which his forgiveness is spoken;
> Your heart with which he now loves.
> —St. Teresa of Avila [1515–1582]

Amen.

e|LIVE

listen|imagine|view|experience

AUDIO BOOK DOWNLOAD INCLUDED WITH THIS BOOK!

In your hands you hold a complete digital entertainment package. Besides purchasing the paper version of this book, this book includes a free download of the audio version of this book. Simply use the code listed below when visiting our website. Once downloaded to your computer, you can listen to the book through your computer's speakers, burn it to an audio CD or save the file to your portable music device (such as Apple's popular iPod) and listen on the go!

How to get your free audio book digital download:

1. Visit www.tatepublishing.com and click on the e|LIVE logo on the home page.
2. Enter the following coupon code:
   5aa1-4a30-f0a7-1470-9898-cdcc-f881-6865
3. Download the audio book from your e|LIVE digital locker and begin enjoying your new digital entertainment package today!